Somewhere in There

FAMILIES LIVING WITH PANS & PANDAS SHARE THEIR JOURNEYS FROM DESPAIR TO HOPE

by
Melissa Nolan

Somewhere in There
Families Living with PANS & PANDAS Share Their Journeys from Despair
to Hope

For more information, e-mail pansandpandasbook@gmail.com

ISBN: 979-8-218-00839-0 (trade paperback)

First trade paperback edition: September 2022

Dedicated to the PANS &
PANDAS community

Table of Contents

*"Walk until the darkness is a memory
and you become the sun
on the next traveler's horizon."*

– *The Wizenard Series: Training Camp*
by Wesley King and Kobe Bryant

Cover Art

My name is Delaney, and I'm 14 years old and have PANDAS. I drew a brain in the center of the painting because the brain is what is affected when an individual has PANDAS or PANS. Surrounding the brain I painted a red circle, which represents fear, anger and sadness. Finally, the bright colors dispersed outside the red circle represent the happiness, hope and joy experienced when a child has healed mentally, physically and emotionally from the hard path they've been on.

Foreword

Sarah Griesemer, Ph.D., Licensed Psychologist

Being a psychologist myself did not protect me from the truly devastating experience of seeking mental health support for my daughter. Before she was diagnosed properly with PANDAS, two psychologists suggested she had autism, one therapist thought she was depressed, and another diagnosed her with Generalized Anxiety Disorder. I've never been so angry and disappointed in my profession.

Yet, I understood. In my 10 years of training to be a child psychologist, no one had taught me anything about autoimmune encephalopathies such as PANS and PANDAS and how they impacted children's mental health. This topic was not represented in my neuropsychology coursework; in fact, PANDAS was only getting a name well after I had graduated. I became an expert only through helping my own daughter. Now, I work with parents whose kids have PANS and PANDAS (referred to throughout this book as P/P) because I want these parents to be given the things I didn't receive: compassion, knowledge, hope, safety, care and support.

4

For those new to it, P/P is a type of autoimmune enceph-
alopathy. In short, this describes a disorder where the body
attacks itself, in this case its own brain, in the process of
fighting a virus, infection, bacteria or allergen. For PANDAS
(Pediatric Autoimmune Neuropsychiatric Disorders Associated with Strep), the triggering infection is strep, although
children with PANDAS can have autoimmune responses
to other triggers as well. For PANS (Pediatric Acute-Onset
Neuropsychiatric Syndrome), the trigger might be a tick-
borne illness, viral infection, or mold or other toxin. While
our understanding will continue to evolve, our current the-
ory is that the self-attack results in the swelling of the basal
ganglia part of the brain. That swelling leads to a wide range
of symptoms, including, but not limited to: Obsessive-Com-
pulsive Disorder (OCD), tics, generalized anxiety, separation anxiety, school anxiety, depression, attention problems,
intense rages, extreme sensory sensitivities, sleep issues,
food restrictions, urinary issues, writing and math regression, difficulty planning and executing tasks, and in extreme
cases, hallucinations and psychosis. Not all kids have all
symptoms. There is no known cure for P/P, though there are
treatments that can help manage the effects and encourage
the body to heal.

P/P isolates parents and ruins marriages in a way I have
seen few other psychiatric conditions affect families. Children who could leave the house, have playdates, go to school
and follow directions are suddenly incapacitated, rageful,

anxiety-ridden, unreasonable, paranoid and homebound. Stressed couples who used to be on the same page with parenting find themselves arguing about how to handle every new and scary behavior. Therapists give conflicting advice: "Don't feed into the child's anxiety" but also "don't push them too hard because you'll trigger a rage." Your pediatrician might not believe that P/P is real, increasing the isolation and confusion and delaying treatment for your child. Families find themselves lost, alone and terrified.

I'm speaking of families rather than focusing on the child with P/P because this disorder is a systemic issue: parents, family, extended family, educators, childcare and neighbors are all affected by this disorder. The mom who struggles to send her child to school because doing so results in the child attacking the parent or harming herself needs support and flexibility from teachers and school officials. The dad who fears his neighbor will call Child Protective Services on him because his child is screaming "Don't hurt me!" needs to know that his family is safe in their neighborhood. The parent who is barely getting through each hour needs encouragement from extended family, not insinuation that this is all somehow a permissive parenting issue. Caregivers who are repeatedly hit, attacked, bitten and screamed at need healing from the very real trauma that their bodies are experiencing.

The dilemma of how to get broader support and understanding is real. How do you explain that your child's rages are not the same as your best friend's daughter's tantrums? How do you talk about what your family is experiencing without shaming or embarrassing your child? How do you convince your child's teacher that your child isn't a "manipulative brat" (oh, how often I've heard this phrase) but is in incredible pain and distress? In the middle of chaos and mental exhaustion, parents are tasked with piecing together a medical and emotional support system that doesn't believe their problem is real.

The challenge of being seen and getting support are the two most common themes I hear from parents: #1: "I don't want to feel shamed for my parenting by telling people how bad things really are." And #2: "Nobody understands how bad things really are." In order to solve #2, we have to start with #1. Our culture tells us repeatedly that there is a "right" way to parent, and if you act in this magical "right" way (that any one of 100 parenting books will claim they are the knowledge givers of), then you can magically control your child's behavior. This way of thinking makes sharing typical parenting struggles difficult, and sharing P/P struggles downright impossible.

On to #2: "Nobody gets how bad things really are." Once parents have a better understanding that people seeing their child rage, or run into the street, or yell swear words *does not make them a bad parent*, it becomes easier to actually share how bad it is. Often the resistance to talking about how bad it is, is the desire for our friends to "just understand" (or what I call, read our minds). We want them to automatically know that when we say, "I'm really struggling" that doesn't mean, "My kid slammed a door and gave me the silent treatment and I'm really mad." It actually means, "I feel so much desperation and rage when my kid knocks over a bookshelf and throws books at his sister that I think I'm going to either implode and hide in bed forever, or explode and might actually hit my kid."

Unfortunately, mind reading—as much as we really want people to be able to do it—is not real. Your friends will not automatically understand that you are grieving the loss of who your child was. That you're wondering if you'll ever see them again, how they were. They will not automatically understand how scary it is waking up each morning with dread, never knowing what the day may hold. How exhausting it is staying up till all hours of the night while your child asks you why this is happening to them. They will not automatically understand how it feels to hear your child say they want to die. They will not automatically understand the deep and devastating loneliness.

If you are interested in taking a step on that journey of authenticity and honesty with those you trust, this book is a beautiful way to start sharing more of your life. By choosing a story from these pages that represents some of your experience, you get to show people a little more of what you are going through without having to say all the words. You'll get to show them that you aren't crazy; that this is real. You'll get to finally be seen.

The stories in this book fill a desperate need for parents, extended family, physicians, therapists and others who work with or love a child with P/P. Though it's easy to find on-line groups and fellow parents who are deep in the throes of trauma, grief, confusion and pain, it is very difficult to find stories of healing and hope. This book offers parents a life-line that we need when we are in the darkest places.

If you are a practitioner, therapist, or physician, I urge you to set aside what you think you know about these dis-orders. I invite you to read with curiosity and openness to what you might understand in a new way. As providers we so often think we know what's true. We think we understand the whole story, but we often don't. The greatest healing we can offer families is through listening and believing.

If you are a P/P parent reading this, I so wish I could hug you and make you tea. My hope is that these stories can help you to feel seen and understood, and give you comfort in a time when comfort is very elusive. Find a comfy spot, cuddle up with your favorite blanket, and read these stories. As you read I hope you can hear these family's voices, and you can hold on to my voice as well. You are not alone. You are not broken. This is not your fault. There is hope.

Introduction

I remember the first time I joined an online support group for PANDAS and PANS. We were still months away from an official diagnosis and my husband and I were desperately trying to figure out what had caused our confident, healthy, happy child to become rageful, anxiety-ridden, paranoid, restless, irrational and depressed. I scanned the first several posts.

Side-by-side photos of a child before P/P and after. Beaming and exuberant on the left, sullen and sunken on the right.

"It's been eight years and we can't do this anymore," writes a mom. My heart drops. It's been a few months for us and I can barely get through each day.

"My kid has been screaming, scratching, biting and hitting everything in her path since she woke up," writes another. "Any advice?"

"If one more person suggests I drag my kid kicking and screaming into school to show him who's boss, I'm going to lose it," a dad writes.

"I feel like I'm walking on eggshells 24/7," says another mom. "We've tried it all: antibiotics, tonsillectomy, adenoidectomy, IVIg and still no improvement. I'm so discouraged."

"I was diagnosed with cancer a few months ago," comments another mom. "I'm on my third round of chemo. And you know what? This is such a piece of cake compared to PANDAS. I think I've cried once about my diagnosis. I cry pretty much every day because of PANDAS."

Tears are running down my face. This time it's not for our child, but for all these children. All these parents. How are they getting up every day and facing this? Where is the help? Why are they coming here for answers instead of going to their doctors?

I don't want to be here, I think. Where's the "Leave Group" button? This can't be our life. But something tells me to stay. A sickening feeling that this is the right group. I tentatively list our child's symptoms. Could this be P/P, I ask? I want people to say, "Nope, doesn't sound like it. It sounds like something else. You need the other support group. The one for Easily Fixed Syndromes." But they don't say that. "Our daughter was the same way," someone says. "That sounds like classic PANDAS," says another.

Where is the hope, I wonder? Where are the children who are now thriving? Are there any? Their stories are also there, I would come to find out. Many parents of children who are farther along in the healing process stay in these groups. They're the ones holding out the life preservers for those still in the deep. The ones who remind us that getting

11

better doesn't follow a straight path. That tomorrow is a new day. That things won't be like this forever.

They're the parents who remind us that watching your daughter walk happily into school for the first time in a year is way better than any perfect attendance award. That hearing your son belly-laugh again is so much cooler than hearing he made the honor roll. That seeing your daughter on a balance beam after a two-year break will feel like a bigger accomplishment than Olympic Gold. That tucking your child into his own bed is celebration-worthy. And that watching your child walk through a door without needing to touch it first is more exciting than watching them walk across a graduation stage. (Though they'll do that, too.)

I'll also come to find out that the same parents who are still in the depths of their own family's suffering are simultaneously reaching out to help others. The same parent posting that their child has again been admitted to the psych ward is telling another desperate parent she's praying for them. The parent up at 2 a.m. with a flaring child is giving another parent advice on finding the right doctor. And so it is with P/P parents. No matter how empty their emotional tank is, there's always time for another parent going through the same thing.

Every so often, when a parent *would* post a story of their child's progress and healing, I would see the grateful responses. "This give me so much hope." "I needed to hear this today." "We need more stories like this." I kept thinking the same thing. We need a book of these stories—to read when we feel like all hope is lost. That's what this book is. It's dedicated to the parents still under a blanket of darkness. The parents and kids who wrote these stories have been there, too. Most would say there were times they thought things would never get better. But they did.

As I started reaching out to the parents who wrote these posts of hope to ask if they'd be willing to share their stories, the response was almost always the same: "I'd love to. Everyone needs hope. Anything for another parent going through this." As the stories came in, I was struck by two themes. The first was that each story was unique in its own way: different ages of onset, different states (different countries even), different ways the symptoms manifested, different ways the kids were finally diagnosed, different treatment options chosen. The second was that, despite these differences, the same common threads united every story: confusion, isolation, loneliness, shame, fear and desperation.

I also began noticing that in nearly every story, the turning point—the moment of hope—came not when the child started getting better. The moment of hope came when one person, one pediatrician, one specialist, one therapist, one educator, *listened* to them. *Believed* them. *Validated* them. Looked at the whole picture. Not one blood result. Not one symptom as separate from the others. The moment of hope came when the symptoms weren't dismissed yet again as "just" anxiety. "Just" depression. "Seems like" OCD.

"Probably bipolar." "Looks like Oppositional Defiant Disorder." "Could be ADHD." The biggest turning point came when the symptoms were finally acknowledged for what they were: the cumulative product of brain inflammation.

This book took two and a half years to put together. At times our son would be doing so well that I'd read the stories as a parent on the other side, nodding at how much things can change. Other times he would be flaring so much that I'd have to put the book on the back burner for weeks or even months at a time. When I'd have a moment to pick up the stories again, I'd read them as simply a parent who needed the hope herself. And I'd remember how far our son had actually come. Our family's story is included in the book, too.

Some names of children and others have been changed to protect their privacy. It also seems important to mention that this book is not intended to be a medical guide. Of course, you'll read how each family sought to help their child and the treatments and strategies that did and didn't work for them. But what makes these disorders excruciatingly challenging is that every child, even within the same family, reacts so differently to each treatment. That's why it's so vital to work with an experienced practitioner who deeply understands P/P.

Lastly, the title of this book came about when we would see glimpses of who our son really was. During what seemed like endless stretches of hopelessness, chaos and confusion, the real him would appear. It was like watching the

14

dark storm in his mind suddenly part, and sunshine would emerge. He would crack a joke, laugh with his friend, give us a warm hug or step confidently onto the pitcher's mound. *He's still in there,* we'd tell ourselves. *Somewhere.* And we'd keep going.

This book is for every family living with PANS and PANDAS, no matter where you are on the journey.

With love,

No Time for Waiting

MOM, UNITED KINGDOM

Outgoing, social and creative are just a few words to describe our 13-year-old daughter, Avilee. In her early elementary school years, she was a busy girl who enjoyed gymnastics, dance, creative writing and swimming. She loved art and had even sold some of her paintings at fairs.

When she was 9 years old, she came down with a stomach bug. Two days later, she asked to stay up to read in bed. When she went to turn off her touch lamp, it didn't feel quite right. So she touched it again to satisfy the urge. Once again it didn't feel right, so she tapped it again. And again. A half-hour later, her arm ached, she was exhausted, and she was overwhelmed by these irrepressible feelings. We heard her screaming and rushed upstairs to find her in a hysterical state.

She eventually managed to explain what was going on, leaving my husband and me confused and at a loss of how to help her. We wondered if it was a sensory-seeking behavior and tried to find something of a similar material that she could touch, but that didn't help. Pulling Avilee away from the light or preventing her from touching it increased her distress. She was in a full-on panic as to why she needed to do this and why she couldn't stop. After three hours of constant efforts, I finally managed to get her to hold eye contact with me while I talked about fun, silly things, sitting on her legs and giving both her hands firm massages. Another hour later she fell asleep.

That was the start of our family's nightmare.

The next morning Avilee felt she had to continue touching anything she came in contact with until it felt "right." It took her hours to get from her room to the kitchen for breakfast. We were all at a complete loss. She found that once she was out of the house, the urge significantly decreased, so we struggled every day to get her out so she could have some respite.

When I contacted Avilee's pediatrician and described the situation, she said the symptoms sounded like OCD and made a referral to CAMHS, our country's youth mental health services program. We were told that she would be assessed in about nine months. And we were simply to wait.

Over the next days and weeks, things got worse. Avilee's OCD became even more intense, barely allowing her to function. It spilled over into school, preventing her from writing and being able to participate in normal activities. She began having an eye-blinking tic and then a painful neck-rolling tic. Shortly afterward she began to have wrist, ankle and side-stretching tics, too.

Her anxiety levels rose and she became afraid of every

black mark for fear it could be an insect. She started getting increasingly irritable, losing her temper quickly. Her emotions were all over the place and not appropriate for the situation. She would watch TV and suddenly become furious, balling her fists and clenching her teeth. She would move from anger to utter sadness, then switch to excitement and elation.

The increase in irritability and emotional lability led to daily rages. These were five- to six-hour episodes where she would be in a never-ending fight mode. There was no rationalizing with her. She looked like a feral animal, roaring or hissing at us. She would scream for hours and was aggressive, trying to destroy things or hurt people. As part of this she started to bite and pinch herself to try to manage some of the tension.

Hallucinations started a few weeks later. The first incident happened after she saw a large spider while in a rage. This quickly escalated to her seeing and feeling hundreds of spiders crawling all over her body. She was terrified and clawed at her skin for three hours. After this first incident she was then prone to hallucinating about spiders on the carpet or walls, and would freeze with fear. She also hallucinated about seeing floating furniture, heads or masks. I was calling CAMHS daily with updates, to which I was told that they would review Avilee's case and see about moving her up the waiting list.

As we waited, one evening Avilee suffered a migraine and

I gave her ibuprofen. A short time later she walked through the doorway into the kitchen. I stood there with my mouth open in shock and blurted out, "You just walked through the doorway." She responded, "Yeah, I know, it's crazy—I don't have to touch it anymore." She was symptom-free for three days. Though it did not have the same magic bullet effect again, ibuprofen continued to at least reduce her symptoms. Long-term use wasn't sustainable, we knew, but this was our first clue that we were not dealing with a typical mental health condition.

A parent on one of our OCD Facebook support groups suggested looking into P/P. I returned to the pediatrician armed with research I had found about these conditions. She referred us to a neurologist, but we were told the wait would take about a year. It was four months after Avilee's onset, and we decided to see a private neurologist. That neurologist ordered an MRI and EEG, and referred us to an immunologist. An extensive array of blood tests was ordered.

During this time Avilee's behavior became too dangerous to deal with ourselves, and a few times I resorted to calling 999, the equivalent of 911 in the United States. Two other times, we took her directly to the hospital. On these occasions she was admitted as a danger to herself and others. Each time, CAMHS was called out the following day for an emergency assessment. Each time, it was noted that Avilee's condition was severe and quickly deteriorating. She was moved to the emergency waiting list. A few weeks later, we got an appointment with a psychiatrist.

Avilee's presentation, the psychiatrist concluded, was not usual for mental health conditions. The acute onset of such severe and varied symptoms made her think that there was most likely a physiological cause rather than a mental health one. When she learned we had already seen a neurologist, she suggested we work with CAMHS to address the OCD with Cognitive Behavioral Therapy (CBT). We were put on a waiting list.

Meanwhile, test results from our private immunologist started coming back. The results did not show any causality for Avilee's symptoms, but the immunologist decided to start her on antibiotics. Her tics immediately stopped. By day three, she walked into her bedroom, got into bed and went to sleep. She had not been able to enter her room for months. All of her symptoms were reduced by half within a week. Her immunologist would later tell us that he almost didn't prescribe antibiotics since the bloodwork hadn't shown anything of concern. He told us it was a good reminder that P/P requires a clinical diagnosis.

By this time it had been nine months. Nine months of locking our car doors to prevent Avilee from jumping out. Nine months of hours-long rages and painful, incessant tics. Nine months of being on suicide watch. Nine months of hallucinations and relentless OCD. Nine months of watching our sweet 9-year-old daughter suffer ruthlessly. Finally getting an official diagnosis of P/P was a huge victory.

However, a month later I caught a virus and Avilee started to deteriorate, with the return of OCD, hallucinations and rages. Her doctor recommended we increase her antibiotics dose, which brought her relief. She still had some residual OCD, rapid mood changes, anxiety and irritability, but they were at a manageable level. Subsequent immunology testing showed slight issues with Avilee's immune system, primarily that she had no signs of immunity from her childhood vaccines.

A couple months after this, her immunologist decided to switch Avilee to a different antibiotic. All of her symptoms returned. I always wonder what would have happened if that had been the antibiotic we had started with. Avilee wouldn't have improved and her doctor would have dismissed P/P as a possibility. It's a reminder how necessary it is for practitioners to try a few different antibiotics when considering P/P.

For a long time, we, as her parents, mourned the loss of our happy, feisty daughter. I have memories of holding her while she cried herself to sleep for months every night, exhausted from a feral rage, begging me to make it so she would never wake again. How do you ever leave those memories behind?

PANS leaves a lasting effect on the whole family. Avilee herself has been through emotions, thoughts and situations that you would not wish on a well-adjusted strong adult, let alone a developing young child. Her younger sister has had to grab hold of her as she tried to jump out of a moving car. She has witnessed her sister in such mental agony that she has feared for her life. She has cried herself to sleep, asking where her sister had gone, who the imposter was, and would she ever see her sister again.

And yet, slowly, over time, Avilee improved. It was never a straight line. With every new virus or external trigger, like a fall that any kid might have, inflammation would occur, and her symptoms would increase again. We were constantly firefighting, never feeling safe or that we could relax. For a very long time she required a constant dose of antibiotics, antivirals, antifungals, anti-inflammatories, steroids and mast cell stabilizers.

Today Avilee is 13 years old and life is so much better. From November to March each year she is generally 100% back to herself. From April to October she flares with hay fever. She still has no physical symptoms of hay fever but we see a direct correlation between pollen and dust and her symptoms.

Despite these challenges, Avilee is back competing in sports, performs in a theater group, and participates in all school activities. During the darkest days, I questioned whether she would ever be able to live alone, if she'd ever complete school, if she would even survive the year. Now she walks to school with her friends and attends all her classes. She stood up in front of her whole school and won a public-speaking competition, and recently performed in a show in the West End in London. Last year she received the most accomplishment points in her school. We know that she has a bright future.

Never give up hope. Find someone who you can offload to without judgment. Find other parents going through similar problems in a support group. They will become your lifeline. Find a place you feel safe to cry and sob: the car, the shower, the garden. You need to let it out. Celebrate every win, no matter how small. Accept that there is not a straight line to recovery; there will be setbacks, but ultimately, things will move in the right direction.

Remember that your child is unwell. It is not bad behavior; their brain is on fire. Let them know how much you love them and you will never leave them. Your child is still in there. Hold on to that and keep faith that you will see them again.

Light Switch
MOM, UTAH

In 2008 we lived in upstate New York and had three fun, busy little kids. Connor was 4 and loved cars, soccer and dirt. Riki, 3, could spend all day on the trampoline or catching ladybugs, and Brian had just turned 1 and was doing his best to keep up with them! One day, out of the blue, something changed. It was like a light switch had been flipped. Suddenly Connor was a different person. He started asking me questions about death in a shaky, scared voice.

"Mommy, if you die, will God let me talk to you again?" I didn't know where that worry could possibly come from. I wasn't sick, nor could I think of anyone close who had passed away recently. At the same time, he started refusing to play outside. When probed, he revealed that it was because he was afraid that there could be poison berry juice that could ooze through the cracks in the sidewalk. If it touched him, he said, he could die.

We were supposed to be starting swimming lessons, which he had been so excited to sign up for the week before. After forcing him into the car and to the pool, thinking that seeing his friends and the water would remind him how much fun he'd have, I couldn't even get him to leave the locker room without his shoes on. He was in utter panic about the poison berry juice that could touch his feet. Needless to say, he didn't swim that day.

That night, he refused to sleep in his bed. He sat on the top step, huddled in fear, insisting that he could see a bear climbing through his second-story window. This wasn't a child stalling for more time. We could see in his eyes that he was truly terrified. It was breaking my heart! What was happening to my boy?

The next day the fears continued. Only now, there were new behaviors. He wouldn't leave my side. When he started making odd confessions to me over and over, I knew I had to figure out what was going on. I can still remember the room I was in as I frantically researched OCD on the computer while he stood next to me repeating, "Mom, my finger just accidentally touched my other finger!" I'd look over at him and say, "That's OK!" I must have repeated that phrase 200 times during my Internet searches that afternoon.

Most of what I was reading was telling me that OCD is usually diagnosed at around age 11. He was only 4! Somehow, in the fine print at the bottom of one of the websites, was a mention that sometimes sudden OCD symptoms may appear in kids as young as 4 in a disorder called PANDAS. I had no idea what it was, but that became the new focus of my research. I found a website that described the symptoms. It was as if they were describing Connor exactly! I knew this had to be what was going on with him. But then I read that it's associated with strep. Connor couldn't have strep, I thought. He had no fever, not even a sore throat. But this had to be PANDAS. I just knew it.

I took him immediately to his pediatrician. When they asked what was going on, I rattled off all the new symptoms: anxiety, OCD, fear of contamination, trouble sleeping, irrational fear of death. I told them I was 99% sure he had PANDAS. They looked at me like I had two heads. They'd never heard of it. So I told them I was pretty sure Connor had strep. They looked skeptical but humored me and did a rapid strep test. My heart almost burst with joy when they came back and told me the test was positive. I couldn't get him started on the antibiotics fast enough. Within three days, he was back to his normal, happy, playful, curious self. I was so relieved. We had our lives back.

Unfortunately, over the years it wasn't always that easy to bring him back from a flare. Sometimes, when the symptoms would return, we knew he'd been exposed to strep, but his throat culture would come back negative. Since we hadn't found a local specialist who understood PANDAS, or even believed it existed, we didn't have access to a doctor who would prescribe antibiotics without a positive throat culture.

Some flares got worse and worse for months while we searched frantically for help. His symptoms would include most of the original ones, and sometimes new ones would pop up, like rage, extreme defiance, mood swings, and re-gression in math skills and handwriting.

Life was hard. School was almost impossible in those years. For months at a time, I would drive Riki and Brian through the drop-off lane, waving goodbye to them as they cheerfully got out to join their friends. Then I'd park in a designated spot and call the front office. They'd send out the principal and school counselor to coax Connor out of the car. Usually it involved me peeling his hands off the seat as he screamed. He would then spend a good part of the day in the counselor's office. I would drive home, often having to pull over to the side of the road because I couldn't see through my tears. I felt horrible. I didn't know what to do, and my heart hurt for Connor.

When he was in the 4th grade, we were able to get him to a specialist in New Jersey who ran a slew of bloodwork and officially diagnosed him with PANDAS. The bloodwork showed that Connor had extremely elevated strep titers, which indicated that he had had strep at some time in the previous few months, and that his body had created anti-bodies to fight it. It was a huge relief to finally talk to some-one who understood our battle and could help us form a plan.

Later that year we moved to Utah, where Connor was able to repeat the 4th grade thanks to the difference in state cutoff dates. He had a bit of a rocky start, but by 6th grade he was excelling in school. He dominated in soccer, wrestling and basketball, some of the same sports we had had to pull him from in previous years due to his OCD and sensory issues. Late in 7th grade he came down with a fever and sore throat. When the doctor informed us Connor's rapid strep test was positive, I'm sure he was confused by my reaction: I started crying happy tears. I couldn't believe he was having a normal immune reaction, with no signs of flaring at all.

Connor is now 17 and a far cry from being the kid his school psychologist said was the most depressed and troubled kid she'd ever dealt with. She had made us feel guilty, like we were bad parents for not putting him on psychiatric medication for his anxiety. She didn't understand PANDAS.

A straight-A student, Connor recently decided to take his GED test to graduate early, as he felt that high school was holding him back from his goals. He is now set to start an accelerated business management degree program. Currently he's holding two full-time jobs, one of which is as a sous-chef at a fine-dining restaurant. There were times I thought he'd never be able to finish elementary school. He's investing, has a car he purchased himself, and has big goals for his future. He's a natural leader who carries himself with confidence and conviction.

If you would have told me when he was in elementary school that this is how things would look 10 years later, I probably wouldn't have believed it was possible. But here we are. There *is* light at the end of the tunnel!

Back to Herself

DAD, NEW YORK

Addison has always been a happy-go-lucky, loving girl who gives our lives an extra spark. She was born with Childhood Apraxia of Speech, a disorder that affected her ability to make sounds and form words. Thankfully, she started speech therapy at age 3 and made great progress. When she began elementary school, she was diagnosed with auditory delays and was set up with an Individualized Education Program (IEP) to help her in the classroom.

Aside from those challenges, Addi grew into a typical teenager who loved soccer, horseback riding, basketball and riding her bike. She was always looking for ways to connect with others who might need a helping hand. One day when she was 13, something changed abruptly and dramatically. After school one day, we asked her to grab an air mattress pump from the basement. She brought up a fan. We laughed. She stared at us, confused. We brushed it off. Later that evening we visited some friends and noticed Addison was withdrawn, not participating in conversations as she normally would have. When we left, she didn't say goodbye either. It just wasn't like Addison, who is conversational and cheerful.

When we got home, she mentioned putting a tampon in earlier in the day. With her strange behavior and the fact that she doesn't typically wear tampons, we suspected toxic shock syndrome. When we started asking her more questions, she kept flatly repeating, "I don't know" in a voice that didn't sound like her own.

We called our pediatrician, who told us to go to the ER. My wife took Addison while I stayed home with our other two kids. The ER admitted her right away, suspecting meningitis. She had an MRI, a CT scan, EEG and a spinal tap. Doctors administered antibiotics and an antiviral medicine.

When I visited her hospital room the next day, it was like 90% of her soul had been ripped from her body. For the first 20 minutes she didn't know who I was. The previous day I had kissed her forehead and told her how much I loved her. This Addison was in a near catatonic state, a shell of her physical being. For the next week she would be visited by multiple doctors, who tested her for all sorts of things. They also observed her behavior: She was suddenly talking in baby talk and had echolalia, a disorder in which a person repeats words and phrases in a meaningless way.

After eight days in the hospital, Addison was put on a strong medicine for catatonia and then released to come home. For the next couple of weeks, she made slight improvements, but also exhibited strange behaviors, like crawling on the floor. Then, her voice suddenly morphed back into that unrecognizable, flat tone and she started emotionlessly answering, "I don't know" again to every question. During this time a couple of different friends mentioned P/P to us. It was among the many diagnoses we were researching and considering.

We took Addison back to the hospital. This time, we wrote "PANDAS" on her room's whiteboard. We were shot down immediately. Because our hospital is also a learning center, a team of about a dozen doctors were assigned to her case: neurologists, psychiatrists, infectious disease specialists and pediatric specialists, among others.

During this second hospital stay, new symptoms appeared. Instead of catatonic, she was hyperactive. Her arms would flail; she would get up and then sit down backward on the couch, feet up on the wall; she did cartwheels on the couch. We would walk for miles around the hospital. She didn't seem to have any awareness of why she was there or of time at all. The doctors asked her several times if she was going to hurt herself and she always said no. But one of the doctors, unbeknownst to us, recorded in her chart that she had answered yes. We wouldn't realize this until much later. We now know to always get hospital reports when being discharged.

By the end of this weeklong stay, we were told by her team of doctors that Addison had bipolar disorder. Addison's grandmother had bipolar disorder, they said, reviewing our family history, and it must run in the family. (We would later come to find out that bipolar disorder is a typical misdiagnosis for P/P.) Addison was discharged from the medical side of the hospital and involuntarily transferred to the psychiatric ward for a mandatory 72-hour stay.

In the psych ward, the baby talk and echolalia continued, and new symptoms also appeared. Addison would sprint to the bathroom because she didn't know she needed to go until it was too late. She would have episodes of screaming that agitated other patients on her floor. She developed OCD with dates. Her cousin would soon be born and she was obsessed with the baby's date of arrival. After the three days were up, we brought her home, knowing deep down the psych ward was never where she was meant to be.

Within a couple of days we were referred by a relative to a well-renowned functional medicine practice that was, by a stroke of luck, located right in our city. They interviewed us and met Addison. They ran her bloodwork, which came back with many abnormalities, and immediately diagnosed her with PANS. They started her on antibiotics and a slew of supplements, somewhere around 15 a day. My wife was amazing at keeping up with which supplements Addison should take when. In fact, my wife was amazing with Addison every single step of the way of this exhausting, terrifying ordeal, never leaving her side. She ended up taking a three-month leave of absence at work to help Addison recover.

Within two weeks of this new regimen of antibiotics and supplements we saw some improvements. Her bloodwork started changing positively. We began to see glimpses of the real Addison emerge. We wanted badly to take her off of the catatonia medicine but we couldn't. You have to slowly, painstakingly wean off that particular drug or there is a risk of stroke or heart attack. It took six months to wean her off of it completely.

During this time, we had incredible support from family and friends. Our other daughter stayed with relatives much of the time. My son spent a lot of time at his best friend's house. Both siblings often had to distance themselves for physical and mental protection from what they witnessed with their sister. My sister-in-law set up an account for friends and family to contribute to in order to cover Addison's medical care, as P/P was not recognized by our health insurance provider and none of the expensive treatments were covered. We couldn't have been more grateful for her and for all those who donated.

We went from a normal family of five to a family who went through hell. It's hard not to always be on edge now, looking for things that might be a sign of a flare. Whenever I hear Addison respond with "I don't know," even when it's in a perfectly typical way, I go back to that time in my mind. It's a haunting feeling. Recently, Addison's PANS team wrote a letter to her school, saying that they've successfully treated her. Reading that letter and typing this now brings tears of joy and fear all at the same time. So happy to read those words and yet scared of the what-ifs.

The truth is, I remind myself, Addison is doing great.

We worked hard to get her physical and mental endurance back to where it was. She missed seven months of school and needed to build up her stamina by returning part time for a while. Addison also completed a neurofeedback program, designed to train the brain to work more efficiently and regulate itself better. This past summer we got to enjoy camping and visits to the lake as a family.

Addison decided on her own to repeat the 8th grade and recently began attending a school for students with learning disabilities. She felt like she'd have the support she needed there. Leading up to school starting, she had a minor flare in which she became withdrawn, tired and emotional. We're pretty sure it was caused by the stress of going back to school. It was a scary time for us, as that was her first regression. But despite that setback, Addi is back on track and loving her life. She is getting back to herself more and more each day. Her first quarter at the new school, she made the honor roll. We couldn't be more excited and proud to see her doing so well.

We truly hope that stories like ours are heard, that practitioners become more educated on P/P, and that legislation is passed to require insurers to cover the costs of diagnosis and treatment. No child should have to suffer as Addi did.

One Who Listened

APRIL, AGE 8, OHIO

When I was 5, I had PANDAS. My parents didn't know why.

I was being so upset and I couldn't make simple decisions, and I was crying a lot.

My drawing and my handwriting were getting bad. My older brother was sad too. It was hard to understand what was happening. A lot of the time I would throw my clothes everywhere. And I wore the same clothes every day to kindergarten.

Most doctors didn't understand what was happening, but one did. When I was 6 my mom read an article on the Internet and found a doctor who can help, so my mom got me medicine, and that got me better. It tasted really bad but as the time went by, I got better and better.

Two years later, I'm almost better. We still take bloodwork sometimes, and I hate it, but I always make it through because my mom always gets me something at the end.

Now I am healthy and happy. You can make it through!

April, now 10, received treatment for PANS for 2½ years. She's been in remission for the past year and a half.

10th PANDAversary

MOM, FLORIDA

Any married couple can tell you every anniversary is special. It signifies another year spent building your lives together. But they will also tell you that the 10th anniversary is a big deal. It represents some sort of milestone. It signals to the world that you have what it takes to handle life's ups and downs together as a team.

When my husband and I were first married, I thought it would be fun to give him gifts each year that reflected both the modern and traditional gifts for anniversaries. It seemed like a really cute idea. For example, paper is the traditional gift for a first anniversary. So with the help of a few bottles of wine and some great friends, I made him a paper chain with a link representing every day that we were married. Each link had a phrase, saying or special memory that we shared. It was annoyingly cute, touching, and a clear sign that we needed to have kids soon because I had *way* too much time on my hands. As the years went on, it got harder and harder to keep up my self-inflicted tradition, and I gave up after about five years. (Don't judge—you try coming up with clever and meaningful gifts for wool or silverware!)

But our wedding anniversary isn't the only one we recognize. Every year, we reflect on the anniversary of the day we first heard the word "PANDAS."

Nine years ago, I started a tradition of writing these yearly reflections, another self-inflicted tradition I would probably fail at after a few years. But I haven't failed yet. Each year I find new and insightful things to reflect on and share. This year, when thinking about what form this year's reflection would take, I couldn't quite shake the weight of it all. 10 years. A DECADE. This year, it's a big one.

It got me thinking back to those early, carefree years of our marriage and the silly tradition I tried to start. Seriously, if I'd kept it up I'd have to get him something with lace and fur for our 13th anniversary. (Although I'm sure many of you can think of interesting ways I could have done that!)

So I went back and looked up the traditional and modern gifts for the 10th anniversary.

Traditional: tin or aluminum

Modern: diamonds

I got to thinking about what these things could possibly have to do with the 10th anniversary of our PANDAS diagnosis, and, actually, the connection wasn't that hard to make. Tin and aluminum are both soft, malleable, non-magnetic, ductile metals. Aluminum resists corrosion and is one of the most useful metals in the world. A lot of those things can be used to describe a P/P parent.

Soft, malleable, ductile: We need to constantly change

and adjust to meet the ever-changing needs of our kids.

Non-metallic: Nothing sticks to us! We let everything slide off because we have to in order to survive this chaos.

Resists corrosion: This disease can try all it wants, but it can't wear us down! We are in it for the long haul because our kids need us to be.

One of the most useful metals in the world: There is nothing as fierce or resourceful as a P/P parent on a mission!

Then there are diamonds. Diamonds are the hardest known naturally occurring material. P/P parents are about the hardest-working, hardest-fighting people I know. But even tougher than us? Our P/P warriors themselves. Watching my kids continue to strive to achieve their goals and ambitions through everything this disease throws at them proves to me that they are hands-down some of the toughest kids I know. And I am confident that at the end of this crazy struggle, they will emerge as the two shining, exquisite, priceless jewels we have always known them to be.

It's interesting how tin and aluminum, described as soft, and diamonds, described as hard, can both so beautifully and simply represent the struggles we face with this disease. It seems like a contradiction to be both hard and soft, but even the contradiction seems to fit.

So this year I am going to be celebrating differently. I could write paragraphs about all my kids have accomplished this year, how they overcame obstacles to continue doing what they love. But instead, this year I am going to sit back, have a couple of beers (from aluminum cans, of course), and wait to see what thoughtful and amazing piece of PANDAversary bling my husband is going to surprise me with for our big day (hint, hint).

Never Stop Fighting
ALEXIS, AGE 15, GEORGIA

Before I was diagnosed with PANS, I was a happy, healthy 13-year-old. I was a great student, a dedicated friend, and passionate about dancing and the arts. After my diagnosis in 2020, my life completely changed. I became extremely depressed and my anxiety was worse than it had ever been. I developed severe OCD, which affected my ability to do small, daily tasks. I began having tics and, within a week, they had spread into full-body movements. I began punching and kicking people, walls and myself, and I almost broke my hands and toes.

From there it only got worse. I started blurting out random words, which then led to sentences, and after no time I was cursing out my entire family with hurtful things I did not mean. I could not control anything I said. I was disgusted with myself for saying such hurtful things to the people I love. I was afraid to be with my friends and family or even leave my home.

I had to drop out of school. I begged doctors to take me seriously and not try to put me into a psychiatric facility. They wanted me on eight new medications that had

40

potential irreversible side effects. I had enough of not being taken seriously and being told it was all in my head. Imagine not being able to control your own body, and every single day you get told that you are making it up and that you're faking how miserable you are.

April 2021, 5 days after Alexis underwent IVIg. She avoided any kind of writing or drawing while she was ill so this is the only drawing her mom has.

After months of having tics, I started having strange, seizure-like activity. I had two EEGs, two EKGs, two lumbar punctures, more than 10 hospital visits, hundreds of appointments, and got more than 90 vials of blood taken. I was miserable. I woke up one morning to work on my online school, and the letters were switching and moving around. I had developed an acute onset of dyslexia and dysgraphia. I had never had any issues with learning, and never had a tic or seizure before all of this. This was not normal for a healthy 13-year-old to wake up with.

After a full year of almost daily doctor visits and constantly fighting for my life, I met someone who would help me. He was a well-known doctor and he spoke to us for hours and listened to how I felt. He was the first person to make me feel understood. I finally felt reassured and not crazy. For the first time I felt hope. I had someone who understood that I truly could not control what was wrong with me. I started IVIg (intravenous immunoglobulin) treatments and for the first time I was capable of reading. I was healing.

December 2021. As she healed, Alexis began drawing again. She astounded her mom when she drew this eye freehand.

Now, at 15 years old, I am almost fully recovered and I have returned to the happy, healthy person I was two years ago. I hope that by sharing my story, I can give some hope to those who are still struggling with PANS. I will continue to fight for the justice of P/P patients because no one deserves to go through what I had to. I have become a better and stronger version of myself, and I am eternally grateful for the battle my parents and I fought to get me here. If there is one thing I have learned, it is to never give up on yourself, and never stop fighting.

In the Rearview

DAD, MINNESOTA

Day 1

I remember it being chilly and overcast. I reflected on the gray haze as we made our way north to the doctor's office, dodging potholes along the interstate. Minnesota always has potholes, but especially so in the spring and early summer.

Quietly, but then with increasing volume and frequency, rhythmic shuffling of paper from the backseat could be heard. "Dylan. Whatcha doin'?" I inquired casually. I glanced over at my wife, Julie, who was staring out the window. We were still processing what had occurred the past few weeks.

This psychiatrist appointment was only the first step of what would become a marathon. We had lost the majority of our 10-year-old son, and nobody knew why. Our rule-following, social, sharp-as-a-tack child with penmanship that mimicked a typewriter had lost his fine-motor skills and his ability to sit still. At school he would sit in the corner with his head in his hands, trying to hold it in. At home the floodgates would open, and he would scream rhythmically, for seconds, then minutes, then hours at a time. He suffered from incapacitating depression. At night, he would rage. There were many nights I fell asleep at our bedroom door, with Dylan sleeping in our bed, to make sure that he couldn't escape or hurt himself. He had tried to do both. We suspected that PANDAS was at the root, but confirmation was still a month or two away.

Again I asked, "Dylan, whatcha doin'?" The rustling continued, louder. Julie peered over her shoulder and gasped. "Oh, no! Dylan! Honey, he's not well." I could hear the manual suppression of fear in her voice. Trying to control the direction of the car and also evaluate traffic, I peered over my right shoulder, but he was too far behind and to my left to see him. I craned my neck instead to the left and tried to look through the gap between the window and the driver's seat. For some reason I saw the floor first and could see his foot. That explained the rustling. His foot was rubbing back and forth on the floor and had trapped a piece of paper under it. No doubt one of our kids' missing homework or some paper that had fallen from a backpack. Shuffle-shuffle-shuffle-shuffle, it went. Like a repeating spasm, or an earthquake.

I turned my neck harder and raised my eyes to see Dylan crumpled in the seat. His head was slightly tossed back, his eyes were mostly white and rolled, and his whole body was shaking. His foot was just the final extension of the tremor that his body was seized with, and that piece of paper was the only signal for help. Panic swelled up.

Julie was stroking his hand. "It's all right, baby. You're

45

going to be okay! Just stay with us, Dylan! Stay with us."

He was having a seizure, and we happened to be on the way to a hospital to see a doctor. We were almost there. "Hang on, Dylan," I said, more for me than him. "We're almost there. We love you!" I stopped in front of the building, gathered Dylan from the car and carried him in the door while Julie parked. I pushed the button for the elevator and could feel his dead weight in my arms. I struggled to keep my hold around him. Up to the top floor, through the doors and into the lobby. The receptionist looked up as I choked back tears and got out, "I need the doc. NOW!" Dylan quivered in my arms, his head limp. Somewhere in my mind I expected a crew to arrive. They would take over. A gurney would be summoned. Maybe an oxygen mask would be placed over his mouth. Little electrodes would be carefully placed that would yield some information, some answer, any answer as to why this was happening to our son. There was none of that.

Promptly, the psychiatrist, who I had never met, appeared before me. I was still holding Dylan. He dryly said, "I'm Dr. Nichols. Please follow me," and smartly walked back down the hall from which he came. Stunned, I followed. We swung into his office. I carefully sat Dylan in a chair and held his hand, fighting back tears.

I listened slack-jawed as Dr. Nichols began recounting his background, where he went to school, who he did his understudy with, and how long he had been practicing. I looked at Dylan. The tremors were gone but he was still un-conscious. I wanted to shove the doctor out his fifth-story window as he droned on while my 10-year-old son was out cold. Was I imagining this? It was like a torturous dream where nothing was as it should be. He made no mention of Dylan, nor of his obvious state. Then Julie rushed in. Dylan came to, twisted open the cap on the bottle of water in front of him, and casually drank from it. It was Day 1 with our psychiatrist.

Day 1,013

The elevator button dings as we head to the fifth floor for what will be our last appointment with Dr. Nichols, who's retiring. Dylan strolls casually into the office, greets him cordially with a handshake and takes a seat. They chat for a bit, catching up on current events, school activities and accomplishments.

For the second trimester in a row, Dylan has made High Achievement Honor Roll. It's his first year back after miss-ing two years of school and being largely nonfunctional. As Dylan rambles on, I can almost see Dr. Nichols admiring the inflection in Dylan's voice and the emotion conveyed as he maneuvers between topics. Dylan is a fun storyteller.

Dr. Nichols scrubs his chin over the remarkable come-back and reflects on their first one-sided meeting, as Dylan lay in his office, incapacitated. For the next three years Dr. Nichols would only witness a fraction of who and what Dylan could be. He never knew Dylan before PANDAS. He only saw a clawing, regressed, often mute, catatonic, psychotic, sometimes suicidal, mess of a boy who wouldn't eat the food he should and couldn't function on any level, anywhere.

Today he sees the boy we've been so tenaciously fighting for. Dylan is loose, smart and engaging. He's a straight-A student who flaunts his dry humor and likes to discuss topics and concepts. He forgets absolutely nothing, just like his mother. It's a trait that is so powerful it will give you goosebumps when he can so adeptly shine a spotlight on a long-ago memory.

In addition to regular visits with Dr. Nichols, we've seen countless others spanning the nation. We've had weeklong hospital stays, several flights for out-of-state specialists, more than 70 infusions, five personal care attendants and hundreds of appointments with dozens of doctors. The contrast is remarkable. From that first harrowing day, Dr. Nichols became an integral part of the team that Julie assembled to get our son back.

We are filled with gratitude and humility for all those who donated, cared, shared, served, prayed and provided for us along the way. We love you, Dylan, and will always keep fighting for you until you are completely freed. We are not done yet, and some days feel like we have miles yet to go, but you really don't know how far you've come until you look in the rearview.

From Pain to Purpose

MOM, MASSACHUSETTS

It was January 10, 2020, when our 9-year-old son, Miles, disappeared.

I expected him to hop off the bus with his usual smile and glee about pizza and "boy movie night," but instead was met with a wave of anger as he pushed past me to get into the house. The intensity of the anger was concerning since we had never experienced this from either of our boys. As the weekend unfolded, Miles exhibited extremely irritable behavior and escalating rage. My husband and I questioned whether something was going on at school, but Miles and his teacher reported that everything was fine there.

The next week I made an appointment with our pediatrician, thinking that maybe Miles just needed some counseling. I remember sitting in the doctor's office studying my son's wide, dilated empty eyes and shell of a body, thinking, "Where has my once happy and healthy boy gone?" How could this kid go from having had the best summer, including attending overnight camp, to becoming so psychiatrically ill that we actually feared for his life? We left the pediatrician that day with no answers and a monthlong wait

49

for counseling.

As we waited for an appointment, things continued to spiral out of control at a frightening pace. Miles' anger turned to outright rage. I kept emailing his teacher, but the report was always the same: Everything at school was fine. He became violent and physically destructive in our home. He made terrifying statements about wanting to die, and then even more bizarre and horrific symptoms ensued. He began screaming and screeching at the top of his lungs, urinating all over our home, and writhing around on the floor like he was possessed. He barely slept. We felt so alone. So helpless. Trapped in a nightmare that wouldn't end.

Super Bowl Sunday arrived and instead of watching the halftime show, we watched Miles rage. Desperate, we called the police for the first time. My body shaking, I remember the feeling of sheer terror coursing through my veins. I was so afraid that this was our forever—our son eternally stolen by an invisible demon and a lifetime of trauma and immense pain ahead for our family.

The days that followed revolved around mobile crisis counselors visiting our home, which only contributed to more stress and trauma. They recommended that we lock Miles in his room, raise our voices and take our "parental power back." Thankfully, our call to the police opened up an avenue of consistent support from our town's very special community resource officer to help us on our darkest days. He became a true ally and friend, so much so that he stayed connected with us even during the brighter days of healing that were ahead.

As a nurse, I had learned about P/P when I attended a conference. I began to fear that's what we were facing given Miles' medical history. Over the following four months, Miles would be admitted to the Emergency Room six times and hospitalized in the psych ward four times. Along the way, we collected the cornucopia of possible diagnoses: Attention Deficit Hyperactivity Disorder (ADHD), Oppositional Defiant Disorder (ODD), Autism Spectrum Disorder (ASD), anxiety, depression and my personal favorite: "unspecified impulse control and conduct disorder."

One of the many maddening experiences was sitting in a meeting with a psychiatrist and social worker at a major medical center. I'll never forget how the psychiatrist sat there as I asked her about different diagnoses. Completely uninterested, she played with her shiny platinum engagement ring and glanced at the wall clock half-heartedly. "This is just a behavioral problem," she said, and "sometimes this just happens to boys." I recall shooting a look at the social worker (who was half my age and had no children) while curtly issuing the statement that "this hospitalization felt like a very expensive babysitter." Let's just say her defensive response was not appreciated.

The sheer exhaustion, isolation, grief and trauma had taken its toll. My husband and I could barely work. I was trying to keep my yoga studio open in the midst of the COVID pandemic while also desperately searching for a provider who could help us. At the same time, I was enduring the very depths of hell that comes with caring for a child with P/P. I could feel my own growing rage burning inside. I found myself trapped in a cycle that vacillated between paralysis and exhaustive action.

We made the difficult decision to send our other son to live with family out of state. I remember flying him down to North Carolina, arriving there barely able to speak as overwhelming grief stole my voice. My nervous system was completely fried. I suffered silently from intrusive thoughts of driving full speed into a concrete wall to end the pain. And yet knowing I'd be causing more anguish to the people I'd be leaving behind was enough to move me away from further destruction. The extreme level of anxiety, depression and Post-Traumatic Stress Disorder (PTSD) was debilitating at times, but in the darkness you hold onto hope and force yourself to keep going. There was simply no other choice.

This deep sense of suffering I was experiencing was all too familiar to me. Thirteen years prior, a motorcycle accident had left my brother paralyzed and three years after that I witnessed his unexpected death. I realized that the agony of watching him die as the nurses and doctors worked to save his life was somehow less traumatic than what I was experiencing as a P/P parent. But I knew I had survived it—as painful as it was. The grief that came out of those experiences had become woven into me like sturdy fibers. Those threads embroidered an expansive scaffolding of resilience around my heart, allowing me to fight harder than I ever thought I could. Deep down I knew that healing was possible and this would not be our forever.

Initially, I relied on my healthcare background for answers and felt immense relief when Miles was finally evaluated, diagnosed and treated by two PANS-literate physicians. But after months of antibiotics, ibuprofen, psych meds and IVIg, we still had no improvements. When both providers had no further treatment recommendations, I lost faith in Western medicine's ability to truly heal Miles from this hellacious autoimmune disorder. I began to rely more heavily on my inner wisdom and faith that an unknown greater force was at play. I knew that the next step forward meant letting go of all I knew and exploring a modality of medicine that went beyond the business of academic medicine and our fractured healthcare system. And so, our true healing journey began. I picked up the phone and made a call that saved our lives.

I will never forget the days that followed. On December 15, 2020, just shy of a year from Miles' onset, I drove to the beach, sat in my car and sobbed tears of joy. It was one of the most cathartic cries I've ever experienced. We were 33 days into homeopathic treatment, and our boy was coming back. There was life in his eyes. There was a calm and loving energy I could feel when he sat next to me, engaged in conversation instead of physically attacking me. It was then that I knew homeopathy was the way for us. Even just writing this I can feel my heartbeat quicken, my blood surge through my body, and my skin tingle as I recall those first signs of healing. Over time Miles went from raging daily to an average of three times a month. He eventually transitioned out of our bed to be able to sleep in his own room, and we now rarely have to clean up a urinary episode. It's felt like one long, slow exhale, with pauses to hold our breath when he has a temporary backslide.

What I've come to learn along the way is that healing is a process more sacred and complex than I was ever taught in nursing school. I've come to understand how an entire family is affected by PANS and how we each have our own timeline for healing, both individually and collectively. As I began to explore my own healing, I allowed myself to fall apart, to mess up, to quit a million times and then start over every day.

I, perhaps like you, have suffered greatly throughout my journey as a P/P parent. There were days I lost hope and wanted to end it all. There were other periods where I self-medicated, numbing my pain with wine, food and social media. It's been one hell of a messy and winding road. Along the way I surrendered to the fact that I had very little to no control over a lot of things, and accepted that all I could control was myself. I knew I had a choice in how I could show up each and every day, and that much of my reality was a product of my own thoughts and beliefs. On the days that

I was not proud of myself and my actions, I worked to be gentler and kinder: starting with me first. Eventually, I softened to forgiveness, which became a conduit for healing and positive change.

Along with forgiveness, I found that allowing myself to be vulnerable, at first with safe and trusted individuals, provided some comfort. But in order to navigate those waters, it was necessary to address lingering hidden feelings of shame and unworthiness. There was much work I had to do on myself and also in my marriage. With patience, compassion and communication, along with faith and trust in the entirety of the whole process, I was able to arrive at the next amazing chapter of my life.

I trusted that someday my story would help someone else, because we are not meant to travel this alone. We are neurobiologically designed to connect, to bear witness to not only our own pain and suffering, but to also walk quietly side by side with one another, allowing space for all experiences to respectfully exist. While our entire family still has some healing to do, I am confident our light will continue to shine, and I know you have that same light within you. You have the ability to do this. You are not alone. This is not your forever, and healing is possible.

Marlena

AGE 15, FLORIDA

The title of this book inspired me to draw this. It represents what it's like to be in a PANDAS flare. I almost feel like a different person, but sometimes a little peep of myself comes out and I feel like me again.

The Road with Two

MOM, OHIO

In 2011 my son, Lane, suddenly developed an overwhelming fear of throwing up. He was just 4. He would ask us hundreds of times a day if he was going to throw up, and none of our answers satisfied him.

Over the course of four months, before anyone understood what was wrong, his symptoms became worse and new ones appeared. He was extremely afraid of tornadoes and tsunamis. He would ask if he was going to turn into a zombie or if his stomach was going to explode. There were constant stomach pains, joint pain, tics, sensory issues and fits of rage. It became difficult to leave the house. If we did, we risked an outburst or an anxiety attack.

I started getting calls from the school nurse to pick him up, as he was also having sporadic fevers and nausea. He barely slept and would wake us up frantic and screaming multiple times a night. It felt like Lane was being tortured from the inside, and we were helpless bystanders. I was exhausted and terrified, not knowing if our sweet, happy boy would ever come back to us.

I happened to be reading *Parents* magazine one day and

came upon an article about a girl with something called PANDAS. I was in complete shock reading the similarities of her story and ours. I immediately called our pediatrician's office for a strep culture and blood test. Fortunately for us, they listened, although they doubted that strep was the cause. The culture came back positive, even though Lane did not have any typical symptoms of a strep infection. The pediatrician was willing to treat him with short-term antibiotics, but recommended we find a specialist for a longer-term solution.

When we started Lane on the antibiotics, we noticed an immediate reduction of his OCD symptoms. He was no longer asking us throughout the day if he was going to throw up, and he was able to sleep without waking up during the night, screaming and fearful.

However, in the following years of treatment, we found it was much more complicated than just strep. With additional testing and the help of other practitioners, we found Lyme disease, Coxsackievirus, parasites and opportunistic gut bacteria. It's like peeling the layers of an onion, our doctors would say.

As Lane navigated elementary school, one of our primary challenges was keeping him there for the full day. He had difficulty focusing in class and would often daydream. His grades suffered, and we had to battle to get him an Individualized Education Program (IEP). Another challenge was that because of his symptoms and the fact that he was feeling ill most of the time, he didn't develop typical social skills. That made making friends very difficult.

At home, he was in so much pain from his gut that a few times he would cry out to me, asking if he was going to die. We were doing everything we could to help him, and watching him suffer was absolutely devastating.

At the time of Lane's onset, our daughter, Alyssa, was only 5 months old, but I started seeing PANS symptoms in her as early as 1 year old. Since I knew the signs, I was able to start testing and treatment for her much earlier. Her symptoms were different. She had OCD related to hoarding, severe anxiety around other children, sensory issues, heat intolerance, tantrums, defiance, rages, night waking and constipation.

Alyssa woke up angry most days and was generally unhappy much of the time. We were always walking on eggshells around her. It seemed that particular things would set her off: a hot car or hearing certain people talk. Any kind of situation that was overstimulating could trigger a meltdown. If we were visiting a friend's house, it would end with me dragging her out the door kicking and screaming because she would refuse to leave. It all appeared to be acts of defiance or control, and these incidents were incredibly embarrassing. She was too little to explain how she was feeling inside, but it was obvious to me that she was not well.

It goes without saying that we couldn't go many places as a family because we never knew which of our children was going to have a problem. Like most parents who are in crisis mode, I was exhausted, terrified and completely mentally and physically drained. I was spending hours on Facebook groups, researching and trying all types of treatments to save my kids. We spent tens of thousands of dollars and they just kept relapsing. Thankfully, we had very supportive family and friends. They didn't necessarily understand everything that was happening, but they were there to listen and pray for us.

After three years of waxing and waning symptoms with other practitioners, we started treatment at a center for integrative medicine. I finally felt like we had support and a doctor who was open-minded and researching just as much as I was.

Alyssa was found to have Lyme disease, Coxsackievirus, mycoplasma pneumoniae, parasites and HHV-6, part of the herpes virus family. After Alyssa's first dose of antibiotics, at age 4, she was like a new child. I'll never forget taking her to a crowded indoor playground anticipating a tantrum. Instead, she played happily and calmly with other children. As the days, months and years went by, there were minor symptoms here and there, but she continued to improve with antibiotics and supplements, until the flare-ups stopped occurring altogether. It was amazing to see a sweet, happy little girl emerge. Everything became less overwhelming, and we started being able to enjoy dinners out, family vacations, school activities and sports. For a while my husband and I suffered major PTSD, always waiting for the other shoe to drop. But the kids kept improving. Six years later, they are still recovered.

We are fortunate that Lane and Alyssa don't remember too much about being sick, but we talk about how blessed we are and how we are called to help other families still suffering. Through the roller coaster of this illness and years of treatment, we have learned so much and have been fortunate enough to meet the most amazing families. It's because of them, our amazing doctor, and those we've gotten to know through online support groups that we have our sweet children back. Our hearts are forever thankful.

Unexpected Compassion

MOM, VIRGINIA

One winter evening in 2019, I had to call the non-emergency law enforcement line on my then 9-year-old. Jesse was hitting, kicking, throwing things, and threatening to hit his sister with a plastic baton. While I called, he locked himself in a spare bedroom. I was embarrassed to have to call the police, and terrified that he might be taken away. But I had to keep us all safe. I couldn't stop crying.

Let me back up a little. For more than a year, Jesse had been exhibiting bizarre and disturbing behavior. He had gone from being a happy, typical 2nd grader to getting out-of-school suspensions almost weekly. On a particularly bad week, he was suspended three times. We had gone to psychologists, psychiatrists, cardiologists, endocrinologists, an Ear, Nose & Throat doctor, a sleep specialist and a gastroenterologist. We even had his eyes and teeth checked.

As I was scanning a parent support group on Facebook, I read a post from a mom whose child had been misdiagnosed with ADHD. The child actually had P/P. I had never heard of PANDAS or PANS before, so I started doing some research. I wrote down every symptom that "fit," and when

I was done, I had three pages of notes that pointed toward this disease. Jesse's pediatrician dismissed our concerns, calling P/P too controversial. We then went to a functional medicine doctor, who wanted to prescribe a mood stabilizer. Then to a neurologist, who said he had no way of testing for P/P. We decided to try our luck with another neurologist, whose practice was more than three hours away. He specialized in P/P and was so kind, understanding and supportive. He had seen many families go through what we had. Finally, we felt like we were making some progress. But with every step forward, there was a risk of a giant tumble backward.

That's how I found myself calling the police on my 9-year-old. When Officer Nelson arrived, he seemed apprehensive, and I felt even more ashamed that I had to call. I imagined him thinking, "Wow, this lady can't even handle her own kid." He explained his hesitation, saying that given Jesse's age, and that Jesse was unarmed, he had no authority to restrain or even touch him. I said I understood.

Officer Nelson then asked what Jesse's disorder was and how it affected him. I was blown away. I had half-expected him to authoritatively tell my son he needed to come out NOW and take his medication. After I tried to explain P/P, Officer Nelson went to the door and introduced himself. He asked Jesse if he wanted to come out and talk. Jesse shouted no. Officer Nelson started asking him what he liked to do for fun ... did he like sports? What were his favorite movies? About 10 minutes later Jesse unlocked the door and then ran and hid under his bed.

Officer Nelson went in and they began talking about baseball. He asked Jesse if he could see his baseball cards. He also told Jesse that if he took his medication, he would give him his police patch. When Jesse took his anti-inflammatory, I thought Officer Nelson would give him a pretend patch he carried around for kids but he took the badge right off his uniform and handed it to Jesse. Then Jesse led Officer Nelson around to see his "treasures": baseball cards, Taekwondo belts, snakeskins and fossils. He added the patch to his treasures.

A few minutes later I overheard my son ask, "Am I bad? Is that why you had to come?" Officer Nelson responded, "You're not bad at all. You just need to work hard to get better, and take your medication when your parents tell you to." He added that maybe he could come back and play superheroes with him sometime when he's feeling better. Before he left, Officer Nelson gave me his card and told me his schedule. He said that if this happens again while he's on duty, to call and ask for him.

He stayed for a few minutes longer to talk to me about P/P and was shocked at some of the symptoms. The reason I'm writing this is to let parents know that there are lifelines. As parents, we can advocate for our kids by visiting a police station or talking to fire department paramedics *before* we have a violent child on our hands. We can explain what happens to these kids and tell them what we need from them.

Officer Nelson said that when he got the call he thought we wanted him to discipline our son, but after arriving realized we just needed someone outside of our family to help calm him down. I am so thankful for Officer Nelson, and glad that he was the one who answered the call that night. While handling a raging, sick 9-year-old was not part of his job description, he did protect and serve our family.

It's been well over two years now, and we have been fighting P/P the entire time. We have made great progress, but still have occasional setbacks. We had to withdraw Jesse from his school, a public charter, since they were not willing to provide appropriate resources. Rather than take legal action, we felt it would be in Jesse's best interest to find a more accommodating school. In his new school, he was given an Individual Education Plan (IEP) and had access to special education within three months. He has been on multiple antibiotics, antihistamines, anti-inflammatories, muscle relaxers, anxiety medications, hormones, and ADHD medication. Currently he is on six different medications, and has been doing well. We are hopeful that he will continue on this path of healing.

Turning to Faith
MOM, MINNESOTA

The summer before our daughter's symptoms began, I remember her running up from the lake at our vacation home. 15 at the time, Kathryn sprinted by me with the biggest smile on her face, yelling, "I love my life!" I knew what she said was true. Kathryn is a ray of sunshine, someone who makes you feel better just by being around them. She finds joy in the littlest of things. She loves people, and people love her.

We had no idea on that trip that our life was about to change. A few months later, in the fall of 2019, Kathryn came down with what we thought was the stomach flu, as her only symptoms were vomiting and nausea. She didn't feel great over the next few weeks, but we figured she was just recovering slowly.

Soon after, my husband and I went out of town, and Kathryn and her older brother stayed back with their loving grandparents. During our trip we received a panicked call from Kathryn. She was in a hysterical state, which was out of character for her, telling us repeatedly that she was going to vomit. I stayed on the phone with her nearly the entire night, as she was convinced no one back home could console her.

The next day, we returned home to a stranger. Kathryn looked different, and she spoke differently. Her mannerisms weren't even hers. She was lethargic and fatigued from the panic attacks she had suddenly been having. She became obsessed with the idea of throwing up, started talking about food incessantly, and refused to go to school. It was like a switch flipped in her, and someone else was now living in my daughter's body. She complained all day of eye pain, stomach pain and head pain. I couldn't wrap my mind around the idea that my sweet daughter could go from being a happy-go-lucky teenager to an angry, irrational, distraught girl literally overnight.

I made a doctor's appointment with our well-respected pediatrician for later in the week. In the meantime, I sat up in the middle of the night researching her symptoms and came across the word PANDAS. There was not a doubt in my mind that Kathryn had joined the lonely and isolating world of this disorder. I spent hours reading about the symptoms, diagnosis and prognosis—it was overwhelming and scary. All I read were horror stories, and I couldn't seem to find any hope or success stories.

The day of our appointment, Kathryn could hardly get out of the car. I felt like I was looking through her. Her eyes were dilated and she leaned against the wall in the clinic. Our pediatrician could clearly see she was sick. I was worried about leading with PANDAS, so I didn't. Instead, I described her symptoms, and he agreed that something wasn't right and vowed to get to the bottom of it. Many medical conditions were mentioned as possibilities, and he explained what he would be testing for. I reluctantly mentioned PANDAS. He was aware of it, but he didn't think this was it. PANDAS typically hits younger kids, he said, and with Kathryn being 15, it was unlikely.

She underwent all the standard testing for every known childhood condition, and all the results came back normal. We were issued anti-anxiety medication and sent on our way. I'll never forget driving home, getting in the shower, and screaming and crying. I felt completely defeated, with nowhere to turn. Was I frustrated her doctor didn't give us an official diagnosis? Was I hoping he had a miracle pill to bring my daughter back? I didn't know exactly what I wanted, but I remember that being one of the many difficult days we were about to face.

I continued to research alternative doctors and made appointments with a different pediatrician, an Ear, Nose and Throat doctor, a holistic doctor and a chiropractor. You name it, we tried it. We were desperate, and it seemed like Kathryn was slipping away more each day. There were days she couldn't get out of bed and slept 12 to 20 hours. The thought of food made her sick. The sounds of our voices would drive her crazy.

Her school was now on high alert, as I had called her in sick more than a normal illness would require. She would try to go to school for a couple hours and need to come home. Her teachers were telling the guidance counselor's office about her sudden change in behavior. We held this illness as tight to our family's four walls as we could. How could I explain to teachers, friends and family that the Kathryn they knew so well suddenly wouldn't eat, was obsessed with throwing up, wouldn't go to school, couldn't solve a math problem to save her life, and was soon going to be put on academic probation?

These were some of the darkest, most isolating days of our lives. We felt helpless when she would tell us that something wasn't right in her brain—like she had vice grips on her head. At times she felt she couldn't survive another day and would say things like, "I can't live like this," or "This isn't fair." The pain was raw and visible and heartbreaking.

Finally, we found a clinic that not only recognized P/P but actually had it listed on their website as one of the conditions they treat. After waiting many weeks for our appointment, we were finally sitting across from someone who understood what we were going through and actually believed how awful it was. Everything the practitioner asked our daughter was spot-on. She validated all of Kathryn's thoughts and feelings, and looked in her eyes with such compassion and understanding. "Many parents and children suffer from PTSD after going through this nightmare," she told us.

It was going to be a long and bumpy road, she said, but she had confidence we could get Kathryn back. She knew exactly what bloodwork to run, what tests to do, and what medications to put her on. She found out Kathryn's strep titers were off the charts and learned definitively that strep was our enemy. We had an action plan and a glimmer of hope.

Even with a medical plan in place, we still had many obstacles to face. We had OK days and really bad days. Since Kathryn looked sick and missed so many days of school and social activities, we couldn't hide it completely from friends and family. To protect our daughter, we were vague when talking about her symptoms, and only a couple of our closest friends knew how bad things really were.

We found that when we did share Kathryn's diagnosis or her symptoms, people didn't understand or believe us. We would receive unsolicited advice about how unruly teenagers could be, or how kids could use a little discipline. They had no idea what they were talking about and had no place in our lives, at least not at that time. I found myself withdrawing from friends and family, as I didn't want to share her story, especially with those who didn't take it seriously. Family members tried their best to support us, but they never truly understood what we were dealing with or how bad things really were.

I also became frustrated with the endless doctors and nurses we would see in the Emergency Room or urgent care who had no idea what P/P was, or, if they did, didn't take it seriously. Outside of our holistic clinic, we never encountered a doctor or nurse who understood the destruction PANDAS unleashes.

The emotional toll that P/P has on the immediate family is profound, too. Aside from what I imagine it would feel like to deal with a death in the family, I couldn't picture life being worse. Our son wanted his sister back, and wanted a parent who didn't eat, breathe and live this disorder. I often feel that he lost his senior year in high school to this disorder, even though he wasn't the one with it.

The financial costs added to the burden. Our insurance didn't cover anything related to "anxiety," so it was up to us to pay for most medical expenses. The doctor's visits, bloodwork, treatments and prescription costs were astronomical. My heart breaks for the families facing the same disorder without financial means. One IVIg treatment can be $10,000—and many times it's not covered by insurance.

We forged ahead with healing Kathryn through holistic and homeopathic medicine. We changed her diet (less sugar and gluten), gave her supplements, removed as many chemicals from our house as possible, drew Epsom salt baths for her every day, and used an infrared heat and chi machine, which helped get her blood and oxygen moving when she was too lethargic to walk even 100 feet.

Being a teenage girl in high school is not easy in itself. Kathryn went through some of the most important times of her life with an illness that nobody understood or could see. We watched as her peers pulled away from her while her school appeared to give up on her. She dealt with endless rumors that she was either pregnant or sent away for treatment.

And yet, Kathryn is a fighter. While I consider our family to be more spiritual than religious, Kathryn tells us that turning to God and prayer during her illness helped her endure the dark times. She did the work, she says, and God answered her prayers. About nine to 12 months into our time working with the clinic's practitioners, we noticed that Kathryn started talking in a kinder tone. She started telling us about her life aspirations and goals, things that had all but disappeared when PANDAS started. She started attending her youth group again. Her empathy toward people re-emerged. She went from hating us, her family, to liking us again. She began to eat more typically and wasn't talking about food 24/7. I never thought she would be able to sit down for a meal with us without talking about how she felt while eating or after eating. Things are still not perfect, but they're so much better. She has a renewed zest for life and is filled with gratitude for her healing.

Today, Kathryn is 17. She went through 18 months of hell with PANDAS but is now about 90% healed. She may always have residual effects, but now she is aware of them and can control them. The other day she was upset, and I asked her what was wrong. "It's just a bad day, Mom," she said. "Everyone has them."

We are so proud to have survived this horrific illness as a

family. We have gotten our daughter back. This cruel disorder couldn't take away Kathryn's love of life. Seeing her laugh and smile and look physically healthy has been a complete joy. She has emerged from this experience with more compassion, more strength and more understanding. She will forever be a hero in our eyes, and I know someday she will do her part in changing the world by advocating for mental health. An intuitive therapist once told her, "This happened for you, not to you," and she now believes that to be true.

Justine

AGE 10, MASSACHUSETTS

2020: Drawn while undergoing IVIg in Boston

Life Today

Deborah Marcus, author of The Parent's Survival Guide to PANDAS/PANS, Texas

Once you are a PANDAS or PANS parent, you are always a PANDAS or PANS parent. My daughters are at around 90% healed, yet the illness has left its mark on every family member, like a tornado leaves a path of destruction. My daughters, now 15 and 13, never want me to share details of their ordeal. They're teenagers. It's embarrassing. I get it. So I share bits and pieces, never revealing who did what or who said what.

Like others, we went through many doctors and many wrong diagnoses until we found PANS and our underlying conditions. Harrowing does not even begin to describe the journey. No one understands it completely except those who have gone through it or are going through it. Telling the story of how it began and how we got to where we are is an emotional experience. It's been over a year since we landed in a good place. I don't remember it all nor do I care to. Reliving it would likely cause PTSD. So I choose to move forward, sharing where we are now, with our children mostly healed, and what you can expect on your own journey.

The imprint of P/P is visible in subtle issues that we face daily. The minute my teenagers are crying inconsolably or acting defiantly, my husband quickly jumps to the thought of whether they are sick again. Whether we are going backward. Whether we will have to relive the awful journey again. Like many, we have to consciously stop and consider whether the behavior is typical for their age or what other reasons may be causing the behavior. My husband, more so than myself, tends to experience PTSD, until I remind him that they are teenage girls, and this is normal.

The girls' lives today are a product of the eight years they were sick on and off. They seem to not remember the worst moments, which is a blessing. Though it might sound like a minor thing to others, it pains me to see how their illnesses have impacted their ability to compete with their peers when it comes to sports. When you must constantly pull your child from their extracurricular activities year after year, it's hard for them to develop and progress in a sport they enjoy. After several years of this, they just aren't able to keep up. Despite their passion for their sports and their diligence in practicing once they felt up to it, they just don't have the experience to make it onto the middle or high school teams.

Sadly, in this day and age, it's very difficult for a teen to start a new team sport. This leads to lots of heartache and tears for them and me. It's not their fault. They have done the best given the awful circumstances. We now find ourselves seeking out individual sports that they can learn and enjoy outside of school. It's not about getting a college scholarship or going to the Olympics. We're more focused on helping them keep their bodies healthy with exercise.

Hidden away from the public's eye are the things they still struggle with. One of my daughters suffers from severe anxiety. When her sister came down with a stomach flu, my daughter had a panic attack with the fear that she was going to catch it. She was scared to leave her room. Together, we got through it. She is in art therapy for her anxiety issues, but this episode made us question whether the therapy is working, or if it is time to search out a new method of treatment. I know she will get better, but it is going to take time and hard work for her and us.

My girls are mostly thriving these days. They go to school and have active social lives. We're still treating some underlying issues, like candida, allergies and dormant tick-borne illnesses. They take multiple medicines and supplements. They are tired of swallowing, drinking and chewing them multiple times a day. I'm tired of laying them out and reminding them to take them. However, we all know that they need to in order to continue to help strengthen their bodies and help protect against future flares.

A P/P family in recovery just keeps going. We address the residual issues. We work on what needs working on. We keep our eyes open for the backslide and keep hoping for a complete recovery. We take the time to help others just starting out on this journey.

For me, the best healing therapy has been using the knowledge I have gained over the past eight years to help others. Daily, I spend time on the various P/P social media pages answering questions, suggesting practitioners, or offering tips for detox, anti-inflammation and more. I also spent a year and a half writing and publishing a book called *The Parent's Survival Guide to PANDAS/PANS* to help save families time, money and tears. There is too much information to try to share in a post or two ... or 10.

Now I spend my time and money sending complimentary copies of the book to practitioners nationally and internationally in the hopes that they'll share the information with their patients. Families need help between the first visit and the next follow-up. I field calls and text messages from anyone who needs help. One call, one text, one meet-up, one book at a time, I'm trying to make a difference by spreading awareness and support.

I wrote a poem that will hopefully help you further understand the feeling of being farther along on the journey to healing.

Grateful

It's early in the morning and the bedroom is silent.
As I open my eyes, I realize that I slept through the night.
No one woke me because they couldn't sleep.
No one woke me because of anxiety or urinary issues.
I am grateful.

I walk to the hallway and listen for my girls.
They are up, on time, and getting dressed.
No complaints that clothes don't feel right.
Not wearing the same clothes as previous days.
I am grateful.

They are getting ready for school.
Eating breakfast, which they prepared.
No complaints that it doesn't taste right.
No worrying about whether it was cut correctly.
I am grateful.

There are medicine cups filled with supplements.
They take them without complaint.
They know they work.
They feel the difference.
I am grateful.

They go upstairs to finish getting ready.
I know they will come back down.
They brush their teeth without it hurting.
They wash their faces, happy to feel clean.
I am grateful.

They gather their lunchboxes and water bottles.
Place them in their backpacks.
Put on any old pair of sneakers.
No care that they are dirty.
I am grateful.

It's time to go, and they are ready.
A hug and a kiss and a goodbye wish.
They happily leave the house,
and meet a friend for a ride on the bus.
I am grateful.

The house is quiet. Just the dog and me.
The phone rings, but it is not the school.
I breathe. My body starts to relax.
Yet still watching the phone and the clock.
I am grateful.

The day flies by and I am happy.
Truly happy. And accomplished.
Without worry, I got work done.
I am grateful.

The school day ends and the buses depart.
"Hi, Mom! I'm on the bus."
I read the text and feel the tone.
Joy and ease.
I am grateful.

They walk in the door and unpack their stuff.
I didn't have to ask a thousand times.
They recap their day and brush off the negatives.
After a snack, they hit the homework.
I am grateful.

Dinner is served and we all eat together.
Just one meal is prepared.
We talk about our day and laugh together.
They prepare their lunches for tomorrow.
I am grateful.

Together, we relax on the couch.
Reading, drawing, writing or watching TV.
After some melatonin, they head up to bed.
By themselves.
I am grateful.

I breathe.
We made it through.
I hope tomorrow is as good.
But for right now,
I am grateful.

Chasing Ghosts

MOM, RHODE ISLAND

It was 2013 when I found myself at the library thumbing through a book about PANDAS. I was desperately scanning the pages for a solution on how to "fix" our son, but nothing sounded familiar. Chris didn't go to bed one night and wake up a stranger to us. He didn't have obsessions, and his health was not deteriorating before our eyes. My husband told me I was chasing ghosts, and maybe he was right. But I was still slipping into a yearlong obsession for answers.

At the time, Chris was 6 and we had already weathered a handful of disturbances, each of which had been explained away by his pediatrician or Ear, Nose & Throat doctor. The night terrors that recently plagued him were apparently from the stress of his impending kindergarten graduation, not from the sore throat and fever he had a month prior. The graduation had come and gone (we sat in the school parking lot when he couldn't go in), and the night terrors were getting worse. He was having two or three a night, and their effects were spilling into his daytime life: He was exhausted and anxious, panicking every time I left the house.

We were instructed by his pediatrician to get him an

overnight sleep study. This only revealed that he was perfectly healthy—no sleep apnea. Today, when I look back at the report, I am appalled by the actual data: It showed Chris was getting minimal to no restorative sleep. But he was breathing just fine at night, so why bother digging deeper.

Instead, we were given a diagnosis of anxiety, and Chris started meeting with a child therapist to learn how to talk down to his "brain monsters" (if only it had been that easy). Our pediatrician also offered an antidepressant, but we declined. He was only 6, and none of this felt right. Dealing a final blow, the pediatrician asked the dreaded question: "Does anyone in the family have a history of mental illness?" I found myself confessing that at age 6, I also had panic attacks and separation anxiety. It eventually went away, I explained, but as an adult, it morphed into generalized anxiety that would rear its head during times of high stress and, interestingly, illness. Sound familiar? After I confessed my secret, it was as if Chris's health issues were filed under the "apple doesn't fall far from the tree" folder. Or at least, that's how it felt.

Through all of these appointments, what was never discussed was Chris's health history. His actual medical file, if anyone had bothered to look, was full of Emergency Room visits and hospitalizations. At 3 weeks old he had spiked a 104-degree fever and was rushed to the hospital for a full septic workup, a series of tests that look for an infection caused by bacteria. This means a spinal tap on a fully awake newborn. He was admitted for five days until the fever subsided. Bloodwork was inconclusive and we were sent home, only to be readmitted 4 days later when another high fever spiked. Chris's first year of life was also riddled with ear infections—10 in 10 months, to be exact. He suffered two ruptured eardrums. By the time he turned 3, the high fevers seemed normal to us. Our house had a solid supply of thermometers and anti-inflammatories at the ready.

Then there was the afternoon he came barreling into the kitchen holding his throat, telling me he couldn't breathe. He was 3. I was able to peel his hand away to reveal a lump along his jawline so big that it looked like his skin was hanging off the side of his face. I grabbed him and my older son, and flew down the highway back to the hospital again. The week ahead was a blur of ultrasounds, bloodwork and a harrowing CT scan. Diagnosis: cervical adenitis, an inflamed lymph node of the neck. Chris's lump was eventually drained under anesthesia and we were sent home with a three-month supply of antibiotics but without an explanation of the cause.

These medical events from Chris's early years were never brought up during therapy sessions or even his sleep study. How were these fevers and infections not somehow related to his night terrors and growing separation anxiety? These questions dogged me, and instinct finally started to kick in. I had to stop shying away from pushing the doctors because I was embarrassed about my own history with anxiety. That's how I ended up at the library surrounded by medical journals that I barely understood and stories of children with abrupt-onset OCD.

Life marched along for us and we started chalking up Chris's anxieties to him just being "difficult" or "overtired." However, after Chris's 11-year-old well visit, life as we knew it would be thrown off course for good. This appointment, on a Friday, included two booster vaccines (DTaP and meningitis). By Sunday night Chris was feverish and complaining of a headache. On Monday, the school called. Chris was having a full-blown panic attack, and I needed to come right away. I took him straight to the pediatrician. After a quick eyeballing of his state (dark circles under his eyes and ghost-white skin) and a glance at his file, the pediatrician dismissed us with, "Maybe he's just afraid of shots." This was the norm for us now. Any time I questioned the connection between Chris's health and his anxiety, I was told again and again that "anxiety runs in families."

That afternoon I witnessed something I had never seen before. Chris sat on the couch and sobbed uncontrollably for hours. I would learn later that, according to the Centers for Disease Control and Prevention,[1] a rare side effect of the DTaP vaccine is nonstop crying for three hours or more. That night, and every night for the following month, the night terrors returned. School mornings became torturous;

---

1   Centers for Disease Control and Prevention. (4/1/2020). Diphtheria, Tetanus, Pertussis Vaccine Information Statement.

we had to scrape him off the floor and wrestle him into the car. The intermittent night terrors and separation anxiety were one thing, but the school refusal was an all-new hell for our family.

I started chasing ghosts again, but this time I saw them for what they really were: our genetics. With the help of a few selfless academics who took the time to answer my desperate emails, I was pointed in the right direction. And that direction was 50 miles north in Boston.

The day had finally come when we were seated in front of a doctor who specialized in P/P. He listened to me rattle off Chris's symptoms, illnesses, lumps and fevers. The whole time he patiently took notes. I readied myself for the mental illness question. Instead, I found myself answering questions about my maternal aunts who had rheumatic fever as children, my maternal grandmother who suffered from debilitating rheumatoid arthritis, and my mother, who had polymyalgia rheumatic, an inflammatory disorder. It was becoming apparent how relevant it was that autoimmune disorders ran on my side of the family. This doctor explained that Chris most likely had a fever syndrome as an infant and toddler. Random fevers and cervical adenitis were hallmarks of an autoinflammatory disorder called Periodic Fever, Aphthous Stomatitis, Pharyngitis, Adenitis (PFAPA). We left that day with a diagnosis of PANS. The next stop: tonsillectomy and antibiotics. The ghosts had spoken!

Chris had not inherited an anxiety disorder. He had

inherited an immune system with a faulty roadmap. Slowly, he started getting better. The night terrors disappeared and along with them, the daytime anxieties. But the years of assault on Chris's nervous system had taken its toll. We had tried talk therapy with minimal gains, but his brain was starting to heal and it was time to try again. Just like a broken leg in need of a cast, Chris's brain was limping along with no strength to manage even the simplest stressors. A year after his tonsillectomy and antibiotics treatment, we were faced with the start of a new school year. With seasonal allergies ramping up and his leisurely summer schedule coming to an end, Chris flared and he flared big.

For the next several weeks we pleaded with him to get out of the car in the school parking lot. He wouldn't go in; he couldn't go in. By week seven of his hodgepodge school attendance, we reluctantly enrolled Chris in a local hospital day program for children with anxiety and OCD. What seemed like a huge setback ended up being one of the best treatments for him. Chris's brain was finally getting the physical therapy that it needed, and for 10 straight weeks he participated in an intensive exposure therapy program. He loved it, worked his tail off and flourished. After all these years of trying to piece together this puzzle, our family was finally coming up for air.

Today Chris is 13 years old. He is going to school consistently. My husband and I can leave him home alone with his brother to run errands or grab dinner. He only has night terrors when he's sick. We know the flares will come, but now we have a plan. We have doctors to call for advice and treatment, and we have a village of families just like ours that we can reach out to. It took our family 11 years to get Chris diagnosed and on the path to healing. We share our story in the fervent hope that it won't take that long for others.

Two Points of View

Mom, California
Daughter, Isabella, age 21

In Mom's words ...

The summer of 2012 will be etched into our minds forever. That was the summer when my daughter's life, and our entire family's lives, changed. Isabella had just finished up 6th grade. She was a busy, social girl, taking dance, guitar and singing classes, as well as performing and writing songs. She was a healthy, happy and kind 12-year-old who had just raised $1,000 for our local hospital.

Though Isabella was normally full of energy and creativity, we noticed toward the end of the school year that she was quickly losing her endurance for P.E. and dance. Her skin tone had become pale and she had dark circles under her eyes. She was also no longer tolerant of the heat. Our family was planning a big vacation to Europe, so I scheduled an appointment with our pediatrician for after our trip. Little did I know that these were small signs that life as we knew it was about to change.

Isabella also started experiencing panic attacks ahead of

the trip. The first episode was triggered after catching a virus, though we didn't make the connection at the time. The next occurred during our family vacation in Greece.

The day started like any other, but I had a strange feeling in my stomach. I ignored it because everything was great—we were in Greece, with family, and all was good. It was a hot and humid day, and I soon sensed that my daughter seemed off. I was in the middle of a warm embrace with her when she suddenly dropped to the hard marble floor of the bustling train station. Her eyes were darting around, and she looked frightened, like she was searching for something, but not sure *what.* She was stuttering, as if someone had stuck a spoonful of peanut butter in her mouth. Then she started doing strange movements with her hands and feet, like she was pushing against a wall. My husband and I exchanged panicked glances as we tried to process what was happening. Soon she began to convulse, her arms, torso and legs shaking uncontrollably.

During a short break in the chaos, security guards carried her to an office. I've always been the calm and collected one in the family, able to keep things in control even in the worst of circumstances. But as she appeared to go in and out of consciousness, I lost it. I was crying and yelling, thinking she was surely going to die. At the hospital, the neurologist on duty kept Isabella under supervision as her speech and ability to stand and walk slowly returned. She told us to run tests on her immediately upon our return to the United States.

In the weeks and months that followed, Isabella, the one who had always been so excited to be at school and with her friends, withdrew. Doctors kept telling us the same thing: Isabella was fine; she just had an anxiety disorder.

But our daughter who was "fine" woke up most days tired and dizzy, followed by one of her seizure-like episodes. She described them as tornadoes in her brain. If she did wake up feeling OK, she had a hard time leaving for school, upset about her weight. She was extremely hypersensitive, worried about what her friends and teachers thought of her. If she could make it to school, she came home early almost daily, anxiety-ridden. She also had OCD, with repetitive thoughts and rituals, like making sure the doors were locked. She had a hard time sleeping at night, unable to shut off her brain and afraid someone would break in. It felt like someone had snatched up our confident and fearless daughter and replaced her with a frail and broken imposter.

We switched her to a smaller school with a less stressful environment. But her senses were constantly heightened to an unimaginable degree. She could no longer do the things she always loved to. Going to restaurants, performing, attending concerts, giving affection and eating were all things of the past. Our daughter who was "fine" had become a prisoner of her bedroom.

Once, when she was invited to a friend's house, she stood in front of the door, unable to knock. She came back to the car. She wanted so badly to go inside, and yet was paralyzed with fear and anxiety. So we drove home, telling her friend's family that Isabella couldn't attend because she was sick. Invitations decreased. It broke my heart to see this girl become a shell of her former self.

Our family was very fortunate to own a business, and my husband was fully supportive of letting my daughter's healing be my full-time job. I was committed to finding answers.

After a few years, the symptoms became so intense that Isabella was becoming unconscious after her seizures and was experiencing even more intrusive thoughts. She was hallucinating and said she felt a presence that was telling her bad things about herself. It was difficult to even get a lumbar puncture to test for autoimmune encephalitis, one of the only autoimmune diseases that our neurologist at the time considered. As the doctor tried to insert the needle to extract the spinal fluid, she jumped off the table and hid underneath it, convinced that the doctor was going to kill her. We were sent to the Emergency Room for the procedure, which was not any easier. She was plagued with paranoia, sure that the nurses were going to kill her if she went under anesthesia.

When we were finally able to get the test done, all results came back "normal." We were left with the same diagnosis of anxiety. But now other diagnoses were being thrown at us, such as conversion disorder, in which you have physical symptoms of a health problem, but no injury or illness to explain them. Though these disorders are completely valid and real, we still felt in our hearts that this wasn't Isabella's story.

Soon after this time, we discovered that Isabella did not simply have an "anxiety disorder" or any of the other disorders that were suggested. Rather, she had PANS. It was at this time that we started identifying what her triggers were and how to start treating them. It took nearly four years to rid her of most of the symptoms. There were days when she would get sick and all the symptoms would come rushing back, and we felt like we were back at square one. Healing was always like going two steps forward and one step back, but she was making progress, even if it was at a slow and steady pace.

All the while, we were lucky to be in a school setting in which the teachers and administration were very understanding and supportive. They, too, witnessed the return of Isabella's health. When Isabella was 17, I remember the freedom she felt to meet a friend and spend the entire day shopping at thrift stores. She was able to go to cafés by herself. She was able to sleep over at friends' houses, no longer worried that she would have a seizure.

In the summer of 2018, Isabella left to attend college 2,500 miles away from home. She was finally healed. She had emerged a young woman who had fought many battles and triumphantly won, taking back her life. She is now a strong, resilient young woman who is equipped to take on any challenge. Parents, there is a rainbow at the other end of this horrible illness and you and your child will get there. It may take time, but you will get there.

Some of the symptoms Isabella experienced during those years were low blood pressure, high cholesterol, pre-diabetes, low vitamin D, high vitamin B12, low iron, fatigue, nausea, dizziness, separation anxiety, short-term memory problems, lack of stamina, insomnia, weakness in legs, heat sensitivity, body dysmorphia, right-side facial paralysis, sensitivity to light, extreme sensitivity to flashing/strobe lights, poor self-image, depression, anxiety, anorexia, OCD, disassociation, suicidal thoughts, self-harm, sore throat, strep throat, feeling sick, feeling of déjà vu, hallucinations, psychotic thoughts, complex partial seizures, psychotic episodes and sudden physical weakness that comes on quickly like a seizure, then goes away like a seizure.

Today she experiences typical college stress, the balance of work and fun, the occasional seizure (the last being October 2018!), and the side effects that come with being a young adult.

Don't give up hope. Though most every P/P kid has their own long list of symptoms, just know that it is possible for that list to shrink. Acknowledge that there will be bad days, flares and scary moments, but ultimately, they will be OK. Never stop fighting, and never ever give up.

In Isabella's words ...

Drowning. That's how the worst periods of my illness felt. As if somehow I had found myself in the deep end of an expansive pool and I could barely move, water slowly filling my lungs. Trying to kick and scream and paddle, but powerless to get myself out. My family grasping out hands to help me but unable to reach me. My friends looking down at me, confused as to why I was drowning, for they had seen me swim before. My doctors looking from afar, with crossed arms and smug expressions, thinking, *Of course she's drowning, but she jumped off the edge herself. She knows how to swim but for some reason isn't.* How could they help someone who did it to herself? There I was alone, isolated in the cold water, slowly sinking, unable to save myself from the chaos that is PANS.

When I use the metaphor of drowning, I don't use it for a spectacle of self-pity or shock value. But rather to explain how helpless it can feel when nobody, not even yourself, can comprehend what's happening to your body. As a result, people assume that a complex and confusing cluster of symptoms must be purely psychological or self-made. And when that happens, you start to internalize it. It's hard for an outsider to truly understand the loneliness and blurry sense of self one can feel from a hard-to-define or hard-to-diagnose illness like PANS.

I remember the first time I felt like a lifejacket had found its way to my struggling body. It was in a quaint, unassuming office on a sunny day in Los Angeles. It was a specialist (to be honest, I can't remember what for), and he recommended a more in-depth test of antibodies. He said something about things crossing the blood-brain barrier and how it could be an autoimmune issue. I had already had dozens of blood tests—what was one more? Lo and behold, it came back positive. Auto-antibodies were attacking my brain. He encouraged us to look into more autoimmune conditions, which eventually led us to find out about P/P and get my diagnosis.

It was funny (or at least curious) that even after being able to assemble a team of doctors who actually believed me, the truth still seemed implausible. So much so that when I was diagnosed with PANS, even I didn't believe it. It took some time to fully undo all the falsities I had begun to believe over the years: that nothing was wrong with me, that my symptoms were made up. The prospect of a future that wasn't filled with struggle or strife seemed impossible. But over time and after getting the help I needed, it didn't feel so foreign anymore and I started acclimating to a life I forgot was possible.

Looking back, I do think of the things I gained: resilience, the ability to appreciate the small moments of life, reasons to be grateful. To acknowledge the privilege I hold in having a relentless support system who continued to search until we found an answer. And to use all that I've gained to propel myself forward, spread awareness, and try to help in any way I can.

The one thing I try to emphasize to other people experiencing a complex disorder like PANS, in which a future of stability feels like a distant inaccessible object, is that hope is something worthwhile. That the isolation and pain are real, and that healing and the unwinding of that pain are not easy, but that they *are* worth it. Hope and the prospect of a messy but full future were the only things that helped to cut through the buzzing of water filling my ears, even if it felt out of reach most days.

Though now I lead a mostly "normal" life, when a flare or roadblock comes my way, I've learned to remember that I'm not trapped in the deep end of my illness anymore. On those days when I'm struggling, I extend my hand, outstretched for the piece of me that still feels drawn to the water, and remember that I can get myself to safety again.

Lena

AGE 8, PENNSYLVANIA

My mad PANDAS face

PANDAS is hard to deal with. It makes you very sad. You have bad thoughts running through your head all the time. PANDAS makes you cry sometimes. But we are brave and we are in this together. You can do it. We will get help so PANDAS goes away.

My cheerful ME face

Spreading Hope from the Darkness

MOM, TEXAS

I was blessed with a happy, energetic, friendly, curious, loving and very funny son. Even at a young age, Matthew's spirit and soul shone brightly.

But as a toddler, my ball of light started experiencing strange symptoms. First, it was myoclonic seizures in his crib. Those were followed by constant ear infections, attention problems, hyperactivity, rashes, eczema, gluten and dairy intolerances, environmental allergies and poor balance.

Unfortunately, those symptoms were only the beginning. Like an awful game of Whac-A-Mole, some issues would subside and new ones would pop up: extreme and painful gastrointestinal issues, diarrhea or constipation, headaches, pain intolerance, nighttime separation anxiety, extreme hypermobility and repeated viral and bacterial infections. Each time a new symptom would emerge, I would be sent home with a different prescription to try – but still without answers as to why this was all happening. I was worried and exhausted, staying up to the wee hours of every night researching.

By the end of the 4th grade, Matthew's list of symptoms was more than three pages long. Some issues were never-ending; others would wax and wane, like the tic that caused him to open and close his mouth.

Unbelievably, life became even more terrifying. After a small ankle sprain, Matthew's pain issue turned into an even more severe and debilitating autoimmune and auto-inflammatory pain condition called Complex Regional Pain Syndrome (CRPS). I cannot begin to describe how horrible it is to watch your child scream in agony when the slightest breeze touches his skin. Because the pain was mainly in his feet and legs, Matthew couldn't walk for weeks or months at a time. He also couldn't sleep, so his energy was shot. This pain disorder would come and go over the next few years.

Those years were spent visiting a dizzying array of specialists – more than 30 of them. Tens of thousands of dollars were spent on tests, treatments and therapy. Finally, thanks to a high-level muscle testing diagnostic technique developed by Lyme disease expert Dr. Dietrich Klinghardt called Autonomic Response Testing (ART), we discovered that Matthew had Lyme disease and co-infections. I was initially shocked since the Western blot Lyme test done by an infectious disease doctor had been negative months earlier. But I quickly learned that false-negatives with the Western blot are not uncommon. After receiving an official diagnosis of congenital Lyme disease from a Lyme Literate Medical Doctor (LLMD), I embarked on finding the top Lyme specialists in the country.

I was a single working mother with an amicable relationship with Matthew's dad, who had remarried and lived in another state. But his dad didn't believe any of it and dismissed my worries. I think deep down, he loved our son so much that he couldn't fathom the idea that Matthew could be so sick. And admittedly, the symptoms did sound outlandish. To my surprise, my sisters questioned me, too. "He doesn't look sick" was a phrase I'd hear over and over. Sometimes they would tell me I was worrying too much; eventually, they stopped asking about him altogether and pretended nothing was going on. I lost many friends, with one even turning me into Child Protective Services. The case was quickly dropped.

Thankfully, the teachers and staff at Matthew's school were supportive. They saw him every day and could see he needed help. They worked to get him under the special education umbrella, which gave him protections and extra educational help. Later, when he could no longer attend in person because of his extreme pain, they provided home-bound services.

I was also grateful to work out a flex-time schedule with my employer. On the days that I had to go into work, there were two wonderful in-home sitters that I could call on to take care of Matthew. In turn they became part of our family.

It was a painful, scary and lonely journey, but one that forced me to become resilient. I dipped into my retirement savings, researched endlessly, focused on Matthew, ignored the unsupportive and negative people in my life, and maintained an almighty faith that I would help heal my son from this serious and mysterious nightmare.

All along, the one thing that blew me away was how my sweet boy handled all this. He was still loving, bright, fun and courageous. But all that changed in the 5th grade. Quite dramatically, Matthew started having extreme rage, anxiety, depression, hatefulness, over-the-top negativity, constant tics and dark, intrusive thoughts. It was like he was possessed. His pupils were dilated, and coupled with his behavior and facial expressions, it was at times like watching someone in a horror film.

He fell slowly into the abyss, worsening with each strep throat infection. He could not tolerate school, had meltdowns, lost all interest in hobbies, raged at and then lost friends, isolated himself from the world, and could not sleep alone. His anxiety was so intense that I couldn't even go to the mailbox without him panicking. He could no longer tolerate homebound schooling, as he started locking himself in the bathroom in a rage when the teacher came. He was also truly addicted to gaming and, unbeknownst to me, even used my credit card several times, racking up hundreds of dollars. Most alarming of all, he started questioning living.

It was during that time that our practitioner, trained by

Dr. Klinghardt, diagnosed Matthew with PANDAS. Keep in mind that Matthew was still in severe body pain. Many days he was unable to walk or stand longer than a few minutes and had crippling abdominal pain along with all the neurocognitive symptoms. PANDAS took all this to a new level, now adding in brain inflammation, too.

By age 11, after a tonsillectomy and many rounds of antibiotics for repeated strep infections, Matthew was experiencing symptoms so severe that his specialists were considering IVIg and psychiatric medication. By this time he was also considered to have high-functioning autism, sensory processing disorder (SPD) and Oppositional Defiant Disorder (ODD).

At the recommendation of our practitioner, we decided to start him on low-dose immunotherapy. LDI, pioneered by Dr. Ty Vincent, uses highly diluted antigens, under the tongue, to build immune tolerance to that specific antigen. LDI is sort of a blending of homeopathy and immunotherapy, though the mechanism is different. There are a broad array of LDI antigens made from foods, chemicals, mold, bacteria, parasites and viruses. At the patient's unique core LDI dose, these antigens are designed to retrain the body to stop unnecessary immune response against those triggers, thus resolving the patient's autoimmune symptoms and inflammation. We started with the strep LDI.

I saw improvements with the very first dose. With each round, Matthew came back to me – the way he used to be!

He even caught strep after the first LDI dose and didn't regress, which was astounding. In the previous year and a half, Matthew had gotten strep 10 times and each time had extreme neurological behaviors, including anxiety, anger and depression. This time, it was a week before I even realized he had strep because he had none of those reactions. To this day, he has not had another strep infection.

I was so impressed with the strep LDI, we started him on antigens to build tolerance to Borrelia and Bartonella, both of which are bacteria associated with Lyme disease. With those antigens we noticed a dramatic resolution of other symptoms, especially with his gastrointestinal issues and the pain in his legs and feet. The striae (stretch marks) on his back, chest and arms started fading. We also began classical homeopathy with an experienced homeopath. The miracles continued. I was skeptical of homeopathy at first but soon began seeing more dramatic results with Matthew, as well as with some of my own complicated health issues.

The bottom line is, there is no treatment as powerful as the human immune system. But when the immune system is attacked by some of the more virulent and clever pathogens (Borrelia, Bartonella, Babesia, mold, strep, etc.), it can become confused and attack itself. These pathogens are so cunning, they can even evade treatments like antibiotics. To compound things, when the immune system is not doing its job, a host of other problems can ensue, including food allergies, gut issues and parasite overgrowth.

After spending so much time with doctors on killing and detox protocols that often made Matthew worse, my whole focus of finding answers changed when I wrapped my head around this: that it was no longer the pathogens themselves causing the symptoms (though they were the instigators), but instead it was the dysregulated immune response causing the symptoms! This was a huge epiphany that would finally put us on the road of recovery and explains why Matthew responds so brilliantly to LDI.

My son was one of the complicated cases, having Lyme disease since birth and being incorrectly diagnosed until he was 10. Today, Matthew is 18 years old and is healthy, happy and achieving incredible things! He graduated with honors with a 4.0 GPA his senior year of high school and is a member of the National Beta Club, which promotes leadership and service skills. He worked exceedingly hard to get caught up in his studies and even earned all A's in dual-credit college courses. Matthew is a neurotypical young adult with interests in technology, philosophy, music and anthropology. He enjoys hikes in nature, which is amazing when I think of all those years he was confined to his room with extreme neuropathy. Most important, his true spirit and soul have been restored. He's happy, loving, motivated and deep, and has that contagious fun-loving sense of humor and demeanor he came into this world with.

Today for me, as his mother, I now feel little worry about his health. Our homeopath is a call away, and his LDI doses are in arm's reach. Most of his LDI doses are only necessary about once a year now, and eventually he may be able to stop taking them altogether when his immune system is ready.

Another important key in this journey, which I whole-heartedly recommend to parents, is manifestation through visualization. Albeit difficult at times, I held a vivid picture in my mind of Matthew in the future being healthy, happy and laughing with his friends on a college campus.

One way I can describe how I feel today is remembering how it felt to wake up on Christmas morning as a child—full of joy, excitement and hope. It's a far cry from how I woke up during those nightmare years. I promised myself back then that when I found answers, I would help others. I have since become a patient advocate and am very involved in the Facebook groups for P/P, Lyme, LDI and more. It's vital for us to spread hope and light from the darkness, and I hope I have done that for you with our story.

Coming Full Circle
JUSTIN, 29, TEXAS

Not too long ago I stumbled upon a quote from an American author named Og Mandino. The timing of reading it and of getting the opportunity to share my story for this book is unexplainable. My mother would call that "a God thing." The quote reads, "Remind thyself, in the darkest moments, that every failure is only a step toward success, every detection of what is false directs you toward what is true, every trial exhausts some tempting form of error, and every adversity will only hide, for a time, your path to peace and fulfillment."

Growing up, I was fortunate enough to be guided through life by an amazing, supportive family that devoted all their time to ensure we kids were in the best possible position to excel in life and reach our fullest potential. In my earlier years, I was your typical kid who played almost every sport, excelled in the classroom, and thrived in being someone others gravitated toward for leadership. However, in 2004, at age 11, something unexpected happened that would change my life forever.

A ruptured appendix of almost three days put me in the ICU. For the next three months, I endured five long,

107

unpredictable surgeries and many hours of agony. I was almost never alone, unless Pops needed to get some coffee in the lobby. After the second surgery I was admitted into the Infectious Diseases wing of the ICU. This meant that anyone who entered the room, whether it be a nurse, doctor or family member, was advised to wear full body protection to limit the amount of potential bacterial or viral exposures to me. When I began having even more severe stomach pain and vomiting, my doctors found out that the rupturing of my appendix had infected my pancreas and had infected my body with strep.

When I was finally discharged, I had no idea what OCD, Tourette syndrome or PANDAS was. I was a 6th grader at a Catholic school. Every day, my buddies and I would eat our lunch as fast as we could to maximize our time to play football or basketball.

One day early in the school year, my life changed forever. I was walking back from the field after lunch, headed to science class, and made my way through the sand volleyball court. I instantly became homesick, depressed, and wanted my parents right away. From that day forward things got much worse. I started developing tics, strange mood swings, and many other symptoms I couldn't seem to control.

Getting dropped off at school by my mom was always one of the worst parts of the day. I instantly felt homesick as she left. Simple things like getting dressed were incredibly difficult. One time getting ready for our 6th-grade musical, I spent nearly an hour putting on my shirt and taking it off.

If I didn't have my backpack in front of me while I walked, my brain would tell me that I was gay since I must "like" the person I was facing. My brain would also tell me that if I stepped on the gray grout between our kitchen tiles, someone from a particular family would pass away and it would be my fault. Almost every night of my middle school years I slept with my parents because I was so depressed and down from PANDAS. When I was with my parents it made me feel like I had some protection. The way I was able to push through and fight each and every day was due to the important impact my parents, family and friends had in helping me in any way they could.

This year I will be turning 30 and I now understand that PANDAS is a part of me but does not define me. These days I am a teacher, football coach and musician, three things I absolutely love to do. Having experienced such life-altering situations at the same ages as the kids I now teach has helped me to become the teacher and coach I am. I can relate to almost any adversity these kids go through because I battled lots of crazy adversities at their age.

In terms of my music, my battle with PANDAS has given me the passion and drive to live my life to the fullest and chase whatever dream I've ever had. I truly understand you can't take life for granted because it can be gone just like that. I still have my PANDAS struggles but I now know that I am in control and realize how to battle it. Anyone who is fighting this disorder and is reading this, please know you are not alone and that you are in control.

Underneath It All

DAD, MARYLAND

After our epic struggle with P/P, I don't think we'll ever see the difficulties others face in the same light. Something changes deep inside you when you watch something so powerfully destructive take over your child, knowing this is *not* your child, but not having any capacity to explain why or how it isn't. Like so many others, our family was completely upended for years as we battled for our daughter. It was a horrible, traumatic experience for all of us. Now that our daughter, Grace, has overcome P/P and become a successful and confident high schooler, we're grateful that our friends, family and doctors can finally see the real Grace we always knew was there.

Grace was spirited even as a toddler. Maybe that's why we weren't shocked as she progressively became more defiant in elementary school and gradually took on new traits like separation anxiety, skin picking, extreme school refusal and ruminating (getting stuck thinking the same thoughts, whether negative or positive, over and over). In hindsight, Grace had several cases of strep throat in elementary school and we now realize that she was getting worse with each bout.

By the time she was 10, she was not able to maintain friendships or be in crowds. Vacations were horrible experiences for all of us, and I still feel very badly for the few times we tried to hire a babysitter and get away for an evening. I bet those poor babysitters are still talking.

Years later, my wife still suffers from PTSD from the daily, incessant struggles. It was beyond bizarre that this sweet little girl could become such a monster and terrorize our household. We had to hide all the knives so that Grace wouldn't hurt herself. We had to lock the car doors so she wouldn't jump out. At times we had to restrain her so that she wouldn't hurt herself or others. When she wasn't being a twister of destruction, it seemed she was curled in a ball of self-loathing and guilt for the way she had treated people. It was heartbreaking.

Both her psychiatrist and therapist misdiagnosed her with bipolar disorder in the 4th grade, and we accepted that verdict. Grace was prescribed psychiatric medication, which calmed her down some. However, when she forgot to take the medicine or refused to, her reactions were amplified.

Then, when Grace was in the 6th grade, a family member saw a segment about P/P on the television show *The Doctors* and noticed the similarities to Grace. Armed with this new information, we went to see a neurologist at our local hospital. That appointment was a bust. Because the symptoms had come on gradually over a few years, and not overnight, the neurologist dismissed PANDAS as an option. Instead, the hospital had a Child Protective Services officer visit us in the waiting room because we had reported on an intake form that our daughter sometimes hurt herself. It was like throwing gasoline on Grace's anxiety fire. Having strangers take her away from us to ask her questions about her harmful behavior just made her even more upset.

We considered giving up on the idea it could be PANDAS. Thankfully we held out for an appointment with a P/P specialist a couple of months later. That neurologist, an hour's drive away in Washington, D.C., knew the signs immediately: rage, school refusal, ruminating, separation anxiety, picking scabs, handwriting deterioration and bed wetting. When she looked at my wife and said, "We are going to heal your daughter," my wife just sobbed. Though it would take a few years to get Grace healthy again, she was right.

I will never forget the day we told Grace that she might have this disorder. A wave of relief passed over her, that somehow this behavior could be due to something well beyond her control. From that day, we started calling any bad behavior "her evil PANDA," as to separate it from her true self. I think this helped a lot, as she didn't want to be this horrific person.

The P/P specialist prescribed antibiotics for Grace. She was still taking the psychiatric medicine. It was incredibly challenging to get Grace to school, to get her to take both medicines, to get her to try to be social with others, and to give her space and understanding rather than discipline. Middle schoolers can be harsh with each other anyway, but Grace felt hated in school. She would bottle up this volcanic emotion at school and then let it out around us each evening. You would not think that a 7th grader would be so strong, but she was often destroying furniture, hurting herself and physically fighting with us. It's mind-blowing to think back, since today as an 11th grader she is absolutely the sweetest, kindest girl that I know.

My wife and I grew and evolved through the long healing process. We stopped "parenting" the bad behavior and gave her as much space as we could, which lowered Grace's anxiety level. By learning not to react to insolence, we were learning to practice peace and patience. Now when we see difficult children, we know just what to say to the parents, and how we can help them.

In the 8th grade we were able to switch to homeschooling for a year, which did wonders for Grace. That was a healing year for her. She had a tonsillectomy, as well as IVIg treatments. IVIg is an intravenous blood treatment, pooled from many different donors, to provide the patient with antibodies that the body isn't making on its own. The goal is to regulate a compromised immune system. I think that being away from the stress of middle school, as well as the germs, helped Grace progress and be better prepared going into high school.

One unfortunate effect of PANDAS on our family was the impact on her older brother, who was in high school during her worst years. For four years he hid in the safety of his room to avoid the chaos as much as possible. He didn't have PANDAS, but did have ADHD, depression and speech issues that we somewhat missed. Though we occasionally took him to a see a psychiatrist, he needed much more, and unfortunately, we missed it because we were so overwhelmed with Grace. He recently graduated college and is just now getting the help that he should have had earlier. The good news is that he and Grace have finally become good friends and stay up laughing and talking together.

We lost a number of years, like many families. Grace is such an amazing person now at age 16. She is grateful to be part of a good circle of friends since she never had any before. She is beautiful, confident, successful, and very considerate of others. Her journey to overcome this awful disorder has given her strength and empathy that I know will serve her well.

Recently we were talking about her college essays, and my wife mentioned that she might want to write about overcoming PANDAS. She stopped and said, "Mom, I don't think I can. I don't remember any of it." Maybe the memories are suppressed because she feels guilty, or maybe the inflammation interfered physically with her memory. We're not sure, but we're glad she cannot remember the things her evil Panda did. No reason to bring that forward.

I sometimes wonder, "What if we never knew about PANDAS?," and I think of all the families who are struggling each day with a diagnosis that just doesn't seem to fit or without treatments that actually help. I wish that we could tell everyone about this horrible condition. How many people see behavioral problems in a child of a friend or family member and blame the parents? I hope more people become aware and can see the struggles others face with more empathy.

If you are in the fog of battle right now, know that many people have made it through, and you will, too. Know that we pray for you every day because we understand. Know that there is still plenty of time for your child to heal and enjoy their lives. And most important, know that this anxious, raging person is not your child, so give them as much space and as much love as you can—so that your child who is buried in there knows how much you care.

Doctor Mom, Detective Mom

MOM, ONTARIO, CANADA

Christmas break, 2011

I had walked into our 4-year-old's room. Jack stared up at me, his big brown eyes blank, almost staring through me. Urine streamed through his pants onto the floor. I remember him saying, "I don't know why I'm peeing my pants." I wouldn't realize it until nearly four years later, but this was the beginning of our journey with P/P.

Developmentally, Jack excelled in every aspect of his life. I considered myself blessed to have a perfect, healthy little boy. From a young age he loved playing hockey, soccer and chess. He'd sit for hours playing with Legos.

During his preschool and early elementary years Jack began exhibiting behavior that could be explained away as "typical" for his age: fear of the dark, refusing to go upstairs on his own, looking under beds and closets to be sure there weren't any ghosts, going to the bathroom two to three times before bed, and wetting his bed nightly. However, over time, the anxiety and rituals increased, and as his mother, I knew there was something wrong. Friends and family tried reassuring me that it was normal, that he would grow out of it. We knew better. Our house was turning into a combat zone, and no one believed the intensity of what was happening within our four walls.

Just after Jack's 8th birthday, our whole world came crashing down. He started becoming violent. At times my husband and I would have to restrain him until he finally calmed down. We were all walking on eggshells, not knowing what would set him off next. Once, we were carving pumpkins and he carved past his drawn line. He became unglued, locking himself in the bathroom for more than an hour, screaming and crying.

Bedtime rituals could not be disrupted. He had to flick on and off the bathroom lights five times, check under the bed five times, check the closets five times, and then begin again.

Then, my worst nightmare. I looked into the family room and saw Jack attacking his 4-year-old sister. He wouldn't stop. I had to peel him off of her and get him out of the house. He had a blank stare in his eyes and was looking through me again. I knew he had no idea what he was doing. He kept repeating, "I want to kill her. I have to hurt her. Get away from me!" It was as if he was possessed. We drove around town for hours that night. Each time I drove closer to our house, the anger reappeared and he continued with the narrative. "I just need to hurt her!" The anger eventually dissipated, and by the next day it was as if nothing had ever happened. My loving little boy was back.

Petrified, confused and beside myself, I knew there was something deeply wrong. No one believed me. He was a perfect angel at school, a straight-A student—compliant, sweet and kind. Playing sports, he was coachable and respectful. Doctors dismissed me and told me his behavior was a normal part of growing up. I tried to let go of my angst and believe them.

Five months later, I picked up Jack from school. Once in the car, he turned his head to one side repeatedly, and his eyes rolled back. As the night went on, the strange body movements continued. He'd hop around, clear his throat and thrust his head forward. Body shakes turned into convulsions. I rushed him to the ER, thinking he was having seizures. For the next few days, every test was run. Not a single thing was found. Once again, I was *that* crazy mom. Within a month, Jack was diagnosed with Tourette Syndrome and I was told over the phone, "There's nothing you can do; he'll grow out of it." Devastation, fear and hopelessness started to set in.

As the months went on, things went from bad to worse. OCD set in even harder. I watched as some friends politely shied away from Jack, and others were downright mean. My heart broke for him. I understood why and yet there was nothing I could do. It was torturous to see him being shunned for something he could not control nor was even aware of.

Anger took over in situations Jack couldn't tolerate: when the bed wasn't made a particular way or when he couldn't flick on and off the lights the exact amount of times he needed to before leaving the bathroom. He would lock himself in, pounding the bathroom walls and screaming at us to go away. Other times, he would hold his head in his hands, angry at himself for not being able to let go of the rituals. One night as I lay in bed with him, he asked me, "Why is this happening to me? What's wrong with me?" Looking at his little face, my heart broke into a thousand pieces. That night I told him Mommy was going to make it all better, and I meant it.

Physicians continued to wash their hands of Jack and imply I may need to speak someone; he was fine and with time would grow out of it. I knew different. I felt it. My boy was suffering from more than Tourette syndrome. Feeling lost with nowhere to turn, I began looking for natural treatment approaches and found a naturopathic doctor. During our first visit she told us she believed Jack was suffering from P/P.

Finally getting a diagnosis, understanding what was happening, and knowing there was something I could do made me feel like I could breathe for the first time in months. To help reduce Jack's inflammation, he immediately went on a gluten-free, grain-free, dairy-free, soy-free, sugar-free and corn-free diet and started taking natural supplements. Within days, the tics dissipated. They returned in cycles, but never with the same intensity. We continued with naturopathic treatments while beginning to move into homeopathy to address the OCD and other behaviors.

For the first time in years, Jack began to show typical signs of illness. We treated his first strep infection with a celebration that his immune system was finally working as it should, responding to the strep bacteria in a physical way—with a body rash—and not through tics and behavior. The second time he got strep, he got a fever and sore throat, more proof his body was working properly. We added a blood specialist to our team who was and continues to be our lifeline.

Jack is now 14 and has been in the maintenance stage of his healing for almost two years. Our blood specialist can no longer see any signs of autoimmunity in his cells. He continues to take daily supplements and eats clean (most of the time!). When he's not feeling right, he recognizes it and will adjust his diet or sleep. He is very healthy and P/P no longer controls his life; he controls P/P.

Last summer, Jack graduated 8th grade with honors, and won student and athlete of the year. He is now a confident teen surrounded by a wonderful group of friends and family. Jack and his sister are typical siblings who fight but love each other dearly. He is very protective of her, watching out for her and making sure his friends do, too. He helps her with academics and has lots of patience with her.

This journey has been a difficult one, and I would be lying if I said I don't worry almost daily. It has been six years since I unwittingly became a doctor mom, detective mom and lawyer mom. Many doors were slammed in my face. In the beginning, I used to pray for a miracle; over time I began to pray for strength and for God to guide me in the right direction. He did just that and so much more. Those days of despair will be etched in my mind forever; that, I know. However, so will everything else that P/P has taught me, like the true meaning of friends and family. We lost some along the way, but boy, did some relationships become stronger. Friends and family picked us up when we were down, celebrated with us, cried with us and felt our pain. Their love and support are what helped me on the daily. The ones who stuck by me, I owe my sanity.

Jack: my firstborn, my reason for getting up every morning to keep fighting and keep searching for answers. He has fought like hell to be where he is today. His determination, strength and kindness have taught me more than I ever thought possible. We are all faced with challenges in life; this was his battle to fight, and for now I am proud to say, he's won!

What I Know Now

MOM, TEXAS

I used to wonder how we would ever heal from the worst memories, the ones seared into our minds. Those nights so traumatizing my husband and I could reference them using only a few words, like "the beef rib night." (Don't ask.) The nights when our son, Michael, would say such depressive, scary things that my ears would actually ache. The mornings he would hide under his covers, refusing to go to school, and demand that I tell him when this would all be over. But I couldn't say when. Only that we were trying everything.

I didn't know how we could ever forget those memories of him raging, throwing heavy mattresses off of frames like the Hulk and threatening to break everything in the house. Until he got sick at age 9, I never knew what it was like to feel unsafe in my own home. During those first scary months, I remember feeling nauseous and nervous as I tried to do everyday household tasks. We never knew what each hour would hold, what might set him off. I remember the crazed look on his face during rages, like someone who suddenly found himself starring in a movie he never auditioned for. I remember how small and scared he'd look after, wanting us to cuddle with him on the couch and not understanding why his inflamed brain had made him do things he couldn't have thought up on his own.

Now I know that we won't forget those episodes, but their hold on us has faded. Now I remember parts but not every moment, start to finish. Now I remember that most of the time, he didn't remember what had happened, even the next day. (A small gift from the thief that stole so much.) Now we savor new memories and experiences and joys, and with each one, the bad memories grow fainter. Now he'll joke about the things PANDAS used to make him do, and we can do the very thing I never thought was possible: find small bits of humor in them. It's cathartic for all of us. Now I know that laughter can heal the areas of the heart that tears can't quite get to.

One of Michael's very first symptoms was intense school anxiety, though we didn't know he had PANDAS at the time. I'll never forget the morning my husband and I dragged him to school, having tried anything and everything for weeks and weeks to try to get him there peacefully. School professionals had advised us that once Michael realized he didn't have any other choice, he would go into school and settle down. They never saw signs of anxiety when he was there, they told us. He always looked happy. They had experience with kids who struggled with anxiety, and avoiding school would only make the anxiety worse. He could sit in the nurse's office if he needed to until he was ready to go to his classroom. It would get easier, they said. He screamed and punched and kicked the backs of our seats during the excruciating five-minute drive to school. School staff members waited outside. In hysterics and after refusing to leave the car, Michael abruptly jumped out and started walking away from us. "Bud, if you step foot off campus, I will have to call the police," the assistant principal told him in a firm voice. I could tell she had to say it but her heart was breaking, too. She would later become one of our biggest supporters.

If in that moment I would have turned just slightly, I would have been able to see the door that Michael had confidently walked through on the first day of third grade only two months earlier. In previous years he had always wanted me to walk him to class. "Do you want me to go up the stairs with you?" I had asked him. "No, Mom, I'm good!" he said, barely turning back.

But of course, I didn't look toward the door in that moment. My eyes were fixated on Michael, and my mind was spinning. It felt like a terrible movie. A school official calling the police on my 9-year-old? How could any of this be happening?

Now I know that the types of treatments you might do for generalized anxiety are different than the ones you do for kids with P/P. Now I know how easy it is to be pressured into doing something your gut tells you isn't right, when you don't have the tools or knowledge or wherewithal to push back. Now I know that kids with P/P often find school too stimulating, too stressful and too unsafe, no matter what anyone tries to tell them to the contrary.

I remember seeing our pediatrician during those first few months. Michael's symptoms were getting scarier by the day. At one of the visits she leaned in. "I trust you," she said. "What do you think this is?" I remember pausing to find the right words, having come across articles about P/P but not knowing enough about it to sound confident. "I think," I started, "it could still be the strep he had a month ago. I've been reading about PANDAS and I wonder … could we test him again?" She looked skeptical but ordered a new test. She returned a few minutes later. "Nope, negative! No strep."

I know now that a child's infection or illness can be gone, but that P/P symptoms can very much still be present. I know now that we have a lot more work to do so that pediatricians will become families' first line of defense in fighting these disorders.

Soon after, I took him to a neurologist. PANDAS, he told us, was still controversial. He didn't think that's what Michael had. He was pretty sure it was anxiety. He offered us a choice: Try vitamins first. Or we could go straight to an antidepressant. We left with a list of vitamins. Our son was barely functioning and now all our hope was in a $5 bottle of magnesium. Until someone could explain to me why our third-grader was suddenly experiencing several neuropsychiatric conditions at once, antidepressants would be a firm no.

Now I know that our gut instincts are gifts to be used. No one knows your child like you do.

Later, when our son was raging every few days, had quit basketball, didn't want to go to friends' parties, had trouble leaving the house, was obsessed with watching the same shows over and over, was saying even more depressive things, couldn't brush his teeth, couldn't take showers and couldn't sleep in his own bed, I took advice from other P/P parents and called the neurologist back. Could we try longer-term antibiotics, please, just to see? He said we could give it a try. For the next 40 days Michael didn't have a rage. Antibiotics wouldn't be the complete answer, but it was a vital clue we needed.

Now I know that other P/P parents are amazing resources. Now I know that we can have doctors on our team for different reasons and at different times. Now I know it's important to keep a good relationship with all of them. Your family's experience and feedback, expressed in the right way, could change their perspective for a future family.

I used to wonder how letting go of all discipline and consequences for months on end would affect our son down the road. We felt crazy dropping everything to go out and buy him whatever food or drink suddenly sounded good to him when he couldn't get the idea out of his head. (I only realized later this was a part of OCD – getting an idea and then being unable to think of anything else.) We were always buying unnecessary things (with express shipping, no less) in exchange for a few minutes or hours of peace. My husband and I would go back and forth in our minds and with each other constantly: He was sick. And yet, this was nuts. We had no rules anymore. There were no punishments for any behavior. Punishments, we found, would only throw gas on a blazing brushfire. Were we encouraging him to be a selfish and demanding adult? How would we ever get back to any semblance of normal parenting?

Now I know that the answer is "slowly." Now I know that the kid who couldn't handle the word no (or any variation therein) thanks us several times a day for the things he has and the things we do for him. He is learning to be flexible. He is quick to apologize. He has an innate sense of right and wrong. He is a leader on his baseball team and encourages his friends. Now I don't have any worries whatsoever that he will have manners and respect in other people's homes.

Now I know that what Dr. Ross Greene wrote in the book *The Explosive Child* is 100% true, though he doesn't talk specifically about kids with P/P. "Kids do well if they can," NOT "kids do well if they want to," Dr. Greene says. When kids can't do well, he says, it's due to lagging skills or unsolved problems. As P/P parents, we can remind ourselves of the truth that sometimes can be incredibly hard to remember: that our child's overriding unsolved problem is the product of brain inflammation. Now I know that dropping all consequences and discipline for that time wasn't just necessary for our sanity: it was the only humane thing to do.

I used to wonder how my daughter, 5 years old when this all started, would recover from watching her brother change so drastically. Too many memories seared into her own mind. Now I know that the answer to that is "slowly," too. And that therapy is important for all of us. Now I see how this experience has made her even more empathetic and caring. And wise. Several months after Michael's PANDAS diagnosis she told us that she wouldn't be going back to our pediatrician if our pediatrician didn't really believe in PANDAS. We listened. Now I know that P/P isn't that hard to understand or explain when you've seen it all for yourself.

There were years when their relationship was so damaged, it seemed the wounds would never heal. She remembered feeling scared and unsafe, and Michael felt he was being blamed for things PANDAS made him do. But those wounds are healing, too. Recently, they both went to a week-long summer camp without any friends and stayed at separate campsites, so they rarely saw each other. It was a huge victory for Michael, who hadn't been to an overnight camp since before PANDAS. When they got home, our daughter, now 9, told me, "Mom, no offense to you and Dad, but it was harder being away from Michael than you guys." When I told him what she had said, he said, "Same. I would see her at the dining hall and wait for her to put her tray away so I could give her a hug." I told him that he was an awesome brother. "Well, she's being an awesome sister, too." How I will remind myself of those moments the next time they get into a sibling squabble!

Lastly, what I know now is that I can know many more things than I used to, and yet P/P can still bring us to our knees. And that there will be days I forget almost everything I know. Because this isn't how things should be. Because all we want is for our children to be healthy and free from pain. And certain things will never get easy to see or hear or feel.

But what I know now is that there are always better days to come. Because better days have already come. Michael is a loving, caring, quick-witted kid. We see the real him emerge more every day. He is an amazing, thoughtful friend. He tells us he loves us multiple times a day. It never, ever gets old. He admires people who have good character and are generous. He just finished 10 hours of educational testing (a huge feat for someone who still struggles with school anxiety) so that we can find better ways of advocating for him this year. He takes his homeopathy willingly, knowing that it is helping his body to heal. This past winter, he and his friend were named co-MVPs for their leadership and performance on their basketball team. This spring, at age 12, he became one of the youngest youth umpires in our baseball league. He sat through a three-hour online meeting to learn the rules. That first game, I don't think he ever stopped grinning. Seeing him out on the baseball field, whether he's pitching or umpiring, is one of our greatest joys. We know all he's overcome to experience those kinds of moments.

One of my dear friends who has been with us throughout

this journey was with Michael recently when he got a splinter in his foot. At first he tried to get it out with tweezers. She told him using a needle is sometimes easier. He told her he was deathly afraid of needles, but hesitantly said OK. She started helping him with it but they weren't having any luck. Then he asked if he could do it himself. As he nervously held the needle and worked to get it out, he would need to stop to wipe tears from his eyes. "I can't believe I'm doing this. I never would've been able to do this a couple years ago." By the time he finally got out the splinter, my friend said she was crying, too. "Do you know what you just overcame?" she asked him. "This was a huge fear of yours, and I just watched you be so courageous and overcome it." She knows this is all big stuff.

So celebrate every splinter removed, every obstacle overcome, every inch forward, every step into the unknown taken. There's that famous book: *Don't Sweat the Small Stuff (and It's All Small Stuff)*. Well, I don't know about that, but my advice to other P/P parents is this: Celebrate the big stuff (and it's all big stuff).

The Art of Healing

MOM, TENNESSEE

This art was created by my 11-year-old son, Bennett. The first self-portrait was drawn when he was 9, at the height of his PANDAS symptoms, and not long before his diagnosis. Since then, he has grown and healed in many ways, and we have found art to be very therapeutic and calming for him.

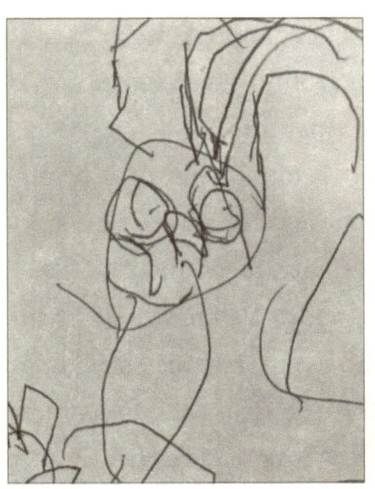 

Bennett's self-portraits, age 9 and today

Bennett was born prematurely at 26 weeks, 5 days, and weighing 1 pound, 4 ounces. He lived in the NICU until he was 7 months old and came home with a feeding tube, oxygen cannula, and 13 medications. Bennett began therapies as a baby and has worked so hard through the years. At age 5, he was diagnosed with cerebral palsy. He has always loved to create but often feels like his muscles are working against him.

In first grade, Bennett had strep many times and had a very difficult school year. He experienced trauma that, along with the effects of strep, left him unable to attend school the following year. As he was homeschooled, we worked with him to recognize and control new behaviors we had never seen before. He became obsessed with washing items such as DVDs, saying they were scratched, and trying so hard to get them "clean." He couldn't be around other kids for very long without being triggered to a meltdown.

In September 2020, Bennett broke out in a rash after playing outside and had a sudden onset of severe tics, anxiety and OCD. He began to experience rages and felt like he was living inside someone else's body. We knew he was still in there but could barely recognize him. He was afraid to go upstairs alone, to sleep alone, for us to leave the house, and more. He used the bathroom many times a day. He ran from us, hurt himself, broke things, dumped baskets of toys. Now he tells us that he was unable to control himself and would feel so sorry after each flare.

In December 2020, Bennett received the diagnosis of PANDAS. He started treatment that included antibiotics, medication to help with his attention and mood stabilization, and antihistamines and ibuprofen as needed. He also began counseling. As he has gotten better little by little, his artwork has improved substantially, and he is so happy his body and mind are cooperating with him more.

Bennett still has flares at times, but the progress he has made has been incredible to see. His art shows that precious, joyful child who we lost and feared would never come back. We hope Bennett's story will give hope to other families.

Keep Digging
MOM, UNITED KINGDOM

I can remember the exact date it started: the day our lives turned upside-down and our happy family was ripped apart, chewed up and spat out, again and again and again. It was a winter day in 2015. It began when our lovely, bright, sensitive, kind 11-year-old son, Logan, had a huge panic attack out of the blue.

He would soon suffer from more panic attacks, severe depression, mood swings, a baby voice, misophonia[2], sharp head pains, rage and other symptoms. We knew that something was terribly wrong but had no clue what was happening. Logan had always been happy, sensible and reliable—such an easy child. The only medical difficulties he'd had were his multitude of food allergies, asthma and hay fever. Our journey, like so many others, has been a very long one.

We were referred to a private psychiatrist, who diagnosed Logan with severe depression and put him on an antidepressant. My heart was broken. How could he be so

---

2   Intense anger, disgust or panic caused by common sounds, like chewing or breathing.

depressed? What had we done wrong as parents? Unfortunately, the antidepressant made things so much worse. Logan became suicidal. When not severely depressed, he became manic. He hallucinated. He zoned out and said he didn't feel real. It was truly horrendous and terrifying.

CAMHS, the United Kingdom's youth mental health services program, told us they could see him in six weeks. We ended up at the hospital with a child who sat in the middle of the corridor and would not move. Coming off the antidepressant helped. We insisted on, and paid for privately, an MRI scan. Nothing out of the ordinary. Over the next months, things started to calm down. We tried to move on, convincing ourselves this was just a blip.

But a year later it happened again. This time it very obviously followed a flu-like illness. This time Logan could say, "It's happening again. It feels like last time. It feels really bad," as he curled up on his bedroom windowsill, hiding behind the curtains. On we trekked, looking for answers and help. Pediatrician again, CAMHS again, counselors, psychologists and psychiatrists.

This time we and the professionals thought he must have bipolar disorder. What else could possibly explain all the different symptoms and mood lability? However, I also began reading everything I could about his symptoms, and came across terms like autoimmune encephalitis and P/P. I asked a few doctors and psychiatrists about these diagnoses, but we were firmly down the bipolar route now.

We had to wait six months for approval of special funding to be seen at a pediatric bipolar clinic, and Logan's depression just got worse and worse. So much of the time he was rolled up in a ball on the floor—I couldn't reach him or help him.

Once Logan was a patient at the bipolar clinic, the practitioners had us try three different antipsychotics. They didn't help, and in fact made things worse. At times, various other possible diagnoses were mentioned, including attachment disorder, Oppositional Defiant Disorder (ODD), Pathological Demand Avoidance (PDA) and autism. None of them seemed to fit. Several months went by and we were getting nowhere. The clinic discharged us, as it was clearly not bipolar we were dealing with.

Around this time, three years after Logan's onset of symptoms, I stumbled across P/P again in more detail, and contacted a pediatrician with knowledge of this condition. This was our first step in the right direction. Logan was first diagnosed with PANDAS, with an allergic element at play, and later with PANS. Though this was far from the end of his story, we were finally on the right track. Simple things like ibuprofen and antihistamines helped more than any psychiatric drugs had. Antibiotics helped—not immediately, but after several weeks.

Today Logan is 18 years old. He's had many flares and remissions. We are now treating him for Lyme disease, Bartonella and Babesia. Logan still suffers and struggles. He was ill for so long before correct treatment. His childhood has been destroyed by this condition, and we can't replace those years. He has had to leave school again, and is bed-bound most of the time. As time has gone on, he seems to have had more physical symptoms: joint pain, evening fevers, stomach pain, weight loss, insomnia and fatigue. His treatment is ongoing, and we remain determined to help him regain some quality of life.

Toward the end of 2019, the worst happened. Our 12-year-old daughter, Emily, our ray of sunshine in the dark times we'd had, suddenly became ill. Her symptoms were totally different, presenting initially like epilepsy. A bubbly, happy, healthy child who complained of feeling a little unwell and went to bed early, woke up the next day with excruciating head pain and dizziness. Over the following weeks Emily began to have what looked like petit mal seizures. The head pain and dizziness were so bad that she had to stay lying flat and had to be helped to the bathroom.

Trips to the hospital got us no further. Her CT scan showed nothing. "Anxiety" had already been mentioned as a possible cause, but we knew for certain that was not the case, and we were determined she would not spend years misdiagnosed and incorrectly treated as Logan had. We went directly to a private neurologist for further tests. By this point Emily was having 40 to 50 seizures a day. Sometimes they were followed by vigorous, lightning-fast myoclonic jerks. They could cause her to stop in the middle of whatever she was doing and drop things, burn herself on hot food in her mouth, fall to the floor, spill drinks or freeze while crossing the street. To keep her safe and prevent injury, we could not take our eyes off her for a single second.

It was absolutely devastating, and Emily was terrified. Sometimes she would come out of these seizures and happily carry on; other times she would be extremely confused and upset. In the very worst episodes, she looked as if she stopped breathing and would come to gasping for breath and crying. There were times she wouldn't recognize me or anything at all for a number of seconds afterward. She began reacting to screens and flashing lights. For months she could not watch TV or look at her phone. Even flashing Christmas lights outside were a problem. During EEG assessments she reacted to strobe lights and TV, but the EEG recording showed nothing.

We were asked if there had been any infection or head injury, but we couldn't think of anything. In retrospect, she had mentioned a very slight sore throat, but nothing notable. We were lost. Blood tests, which took a few months, as the first nurses had been unable to draw blood, showed high levels of streptococcus and mycoplasma bacteria: a lightbulb moment for us. This looked to be along the lines of what had happened to our son, but the presentation was completely different.

The first antibiotics Emily was prescribed did very little. However, a course of steroids, prescribed for possible chorea[3], miraculously got rid of the screen and flashing light difficulties, and she could finally watch TV again! But nighttime seizures persisted, and we became almost nocturnal. In the evenings she would get bright red cheeks, start to feel unwell, perhaps with a headache or sore throat, and then the seizures would begin. They would keep us all up until 3 or 4 in the morning.

I would lie next to Emily and we would try to keep busy, distracting ourselves with drawing or card games, all the while staying horizontal due to her dizziness. I would have to drag her to the bathroom on a duvet and sit with her. I honestly cannot believe that we got through those times.

Eventually, under the care of a private doctor, and with further blood tests still showing high streptococcus titers, we switched antibiotics. Two weeks later, the seizures stopped completely. It was the moment we'd been dreaming of. We had eight blissful weeks seizure-free. We slept. We began to relax. Our daughter was able to return to school.

Unfortunately, even though she was still on antibiotics, Emily began to develop recurrent tonsilitis. When we would try to reduce the dose, she would develop tonsilitis symptoms—sore throat, headache, white spots where her tonsils were—and then seizures! We would change antibiotics again and again until we found one that worked. Each time, once the tonsilitis resolved, so did the seizures. She also had her

---

3   A neurological disorder characterized by involuntary movements that are not repetitive or rhythmic.

tonsils and adenoids removed in the hope that her bacterial load would ease and make infections easier to control.

She has a residual high heart rate and histamine issues, which we believe have been triggered by or worsened by continued infection and immune dysfunction. We feel lucky that she is getting good medical care for such a complex condition, and are very fortunate to be able to access it privately. I dread to think what would have happened otherwise.

Today, Emily is 13 and attends school full time. She has friends, plays sports, and is amazingly resilient and determined. She still takes antibiotics and anti-inflammatories and tires easily, so we make sure to have restful weekends and pace ourselves. She has not had a seizure in almost a year. She continues to get strep infections, but they aren't causing other symptoms and recently they haven't caused full-blown tonsilitis.

I would do anything to have two well, happy children. Sometimes I don't know how we keep going! Seeing Emily doing so well helps. Occasional smiles from Logan help. We have two dogs we all adore and they help the kids so much. Just walking them in the sun is my reprieve. My husband is great, too, and we have stuck firmly together to get through this as a team. I have one wonderful friend who is also a lifeline.

Like most P/P parents will tell you, never give up. Keep digging for the root causes. Even if you've found one triggering infection or cause of inflammation, there may be others.

Keep an open mind. Follow your gut. Strep, like other bacteria, can be resistant to some antibiotics, so try a different one if you aren't getting anywhere. Always consider that Lyme and Bartonella could be involved, even if you never saw a rash or tick bite or cat scratch. Research, research, research.

What I Remember Most

KATE, AGE 13, TEXAS

To be honest, I don't remember much about my PANDAS attacks at all. I know the basics: They always ended in destruction, and they made me seem like a monster. According to my mom, I was diagnosed when I was 5 years old, at the end of kindergarten, but she says my rages had been going on long before that. I don't think I ever had one at school. I do remember doing everything in my power to keep it that way. I was absolutely terrified that it would happen.

The flare I remember most was my worst one. It was the night after I had gotten my tonsils removed. I think the surgery was to try to help me sleep. After the surgery, I refused to take my painkillers or eat or drink or sleep. The thing I remember most were the sleepless nights after the surgery in which my dad did everything in his power to get me to sleep. I remember passing out inside a Thomas the Tank Engine tent one day after having a tantrum. My dad tried to re-create that night because I had finally slept. I remember laying inside the tent, watching a *Wild Kratts* episode, and feeling purely exhausted. I don't know if I fell asleep. Not long after that, I remember my dad taking me to the hospital and having to stay there so they could pump fluids into my dehydrated self.

The thing that seemed to be the most common occurrence in my attacks was the throwing of my mattress across my room. I remember struggling to get the mattress off of my bed to throw it onto the floor. Quite a few times, I would crawl underneath it because I liked the feel of the weight.

Clothes also never seemed to feel right. They were always too tight, too loose, too clingy, too soft, too rough. That still happens a lot today. I will often end up changing multiple times, trying to find clothes that feel right. Nowadays, flares are better. Like, a lot better. I don't think I have had one in almost two years now. This could be that because of the pandemic lockdown, I haven't had strep, but I like to think that it is because it is getting better. I am off all of my medicine that I was taking. I do miss taking gabapentin (an anti-convulsant), because my dad and dog were also taking it at the time, and I thought that was funny. It's nice to not have to worry about taking my meds, and it has made sleepovers easier. I am in a very different place now, and that is a great thing.

A Q&A between Kate and her mom:

Mom: How did our responses, as your parents, affect you when you were little and had flares?

Kate: Kind of annoying, because you'd try to be with me when I wanted to be alone, but I couldn't communicate that in the moment because my brain wasn't working for me to talk.

Mom: Did having PANDAS ever make you feel bad about yourself?

Kate: Yes, it did, actually. I was super embarrassed about it. I never told anyone at school for a long time. People found out accidentally and I felt embarrassed at first that they knew, but they were actually super understanding about it, and life went back to normal pretty quickly.

Mom: Do you remember the school doing anything that was helpful?

Kate: I remember they let me bring my stuffy to school to keep with me, and that helped a lot.

Mom: If you could go back in time and have us do something different, what would you change?

Kate: I would not have us do that tonsil surgery because afterward we had to go back to the hospital again and it was so bad because I wouldn't take my pain meds.

Mom: What do you think was your most helpful skill you used when you were little to manage your PANDAS feelings?

Kate: Being able to hide. It really helped to be able to be in my room and alone for a while when I was overwhelmed, even if I was destroying stuff. Sometimes I liked to just be in my room and sometimes I needed to hide in the closet or under the mattress or under the bed.

Mom: What would you tell a kid who had just been diagnosed?

Kate: The world isn't ending. It will get better as you get older. One thing that was really helpful was to get me on medicine. It helped a lot. Also, therapy helped a lot. In therapy we created names for the parts inside of me that controlled the things that I did. My brain we called Puppy, and it was an imaginary dog that lived inside me and took care of me. The PANDAS part was called Worry Bully because it made me worry a lot. My therapist and I imagined it as a dinosaur because it looked scary. It was helpful to have the different parts named because it let me understand how there were different parts of me doing different things, and it helped me to know how to help myself.

Sydney

AGE 13, OREGON

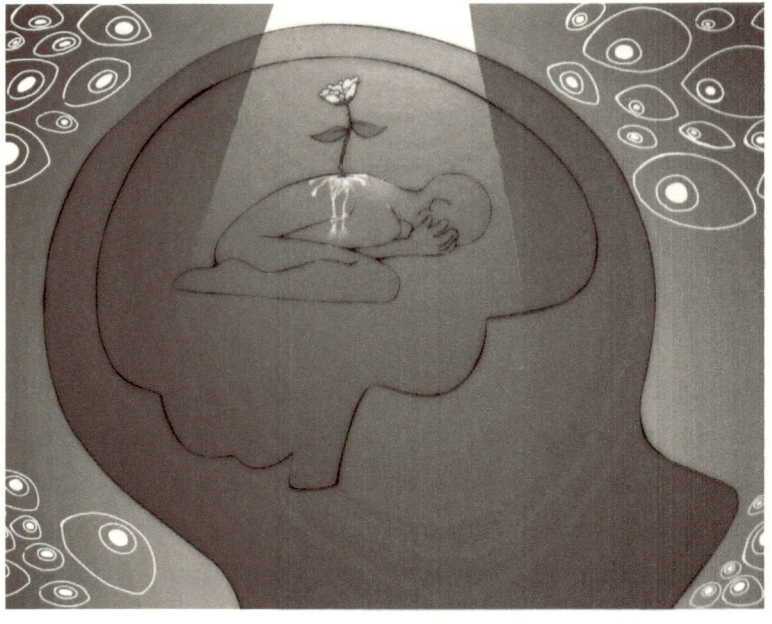

I was diagnosed with PANDAS when I was 6 and had symptoms until I was 11. When I was having symptoms, I felt like I was trapped inside of my own brain, but now that I'm in remission, I feel like I'm myself again—that I have control over my emotions.

I wish I knew not to give up hope. Sometimes when I was struggling with PANDAS, I felt like the world was collapsing in on me, and I just wanted to let it crumble, but I think not giving up hope and being strong was part of the reason I made it to the point I'm at now.

I know you may seem lost, like you're running through a maze with no end, but there is an end—you just have to keep running to find it. It may be tiring, but you will eventually get to the end, and the whole world will open up to you.

Life in Color

MOM, MISSOURI

Nick is a sweet and considerate 9-year-old boy who has always had challenges tolerating change and calming down when he is upset. I received a lot of advice about how to handle him. I was constantly told to give it time and he'd grow out of it, but that rarely happened. I was often accused of spoiling him and was told I created this behavior by allowing him to be clingy. My gut told me something else was at play, but my mind started to doubt.

I chalked up his resistance to change to all the transitions he had had in his short life, including three moves in five years and the challenges that come with new siblings (he's the oldest of four). When it came time for kindergarten, we decided to homeschool Nick, as I didn't think a classroom was the right place for him.

We tried play therapy to address some of our concerns. It took Nick about a month to feel comfortable enough with the therapist that he didn't need me in the room. Then we had a round of colds go through the house, and Nick refused to work with the therapist after that. She told us he was a highly sensitive child, which explained a lot of things, but not everything. After our most recent move we had another round of colds and decided to put a temporary hold on play therapy.

Not long after this, the pandemic occurred, and being at home gave me a chance to try to figure out more about Nick. Things continued to go downhill. He had a worsening tic (neck twitching) and was having horrible rages. He started saying he wished he'd never been born, and began having intrusive and inappropriate thoughts for his age. He also was struggling with learning. He could read, but couldn't comprehend much of what he was reading and refused to write anything. If he tried something new and it didn't work, he wouldn't try again. He would paint something and then color it all in black.

I was looking at each symptom separately and was lost as to what was going on. I read about highly sensitive kids. Some of that seemed to fit and some didn't. I read about bipolar disorder, and that too didn't quite fit. One day I asked a friend to pray for Nick and told her more about his struggles. She told me that when her OCD flares, she has intrusive thoughts. I researched OCD in children and found a connection to P/P. Everything I read fit what we were seeing. It also explained why Nick struggled with writing and why he would get so frustrated with not being perfect the first time he did something. Anytime he caught a cold, his body would flare, which explains why he regressed in play therapy after being sick.

Praise God, I finally had somewhere to start! I knew in my heart this was it, but I wanted to know for sure. Nick underwent Meridian Stress Assessment, a form of bioenergetic testing that aims to detect energetic and regulatory disturbances in the body. Working with the practitioner revealed that Nick had strep in his brain (it had passed the blood brain barrier). Instantly, my heart sank because I knew I had passed Group C strep to Nick in utero. He had been born with a blood infection and almost died. But I also had immense relief that we now had some answers.

He started some homeopathy and an herbal remedy while I started researching everything I could. We could go one of two ways with his treatment: natural (homeopathy, herbs, diet and supplements to support the body and make it stronger to fight the strep while we cleared it), or the most widely accepted method of antibiotics and steroids.

We chose the natural way for several reasons. The homeopathy and herbal remedy were already working. I saw a change very quickly in his rage. I also found a chiropractor who specializes in children with P/P and other hidden infections. Not only were his tics going away, but his intrusive thoughts were less frequent and he was able to better control his anger and rages. He also started writing, drawing and painting with Lily, our second-oldest, and even started riding a bike. Prior to his treatment he wouldn't do any of those things and would become very angry if pushed. I was planning to have him evaluated for dysgraphia before all of this. There have been so many improvements since then. I mentioned some of the big ones, but there have been many more small changes we've seen, too.

Lily, at this time 6 years old, also underwent Meridian Stress Assessment, and strep was found in her brain, too. C. diff, a bacterium that causes severe diarrhea, was also found. By the time she was about 7, she started having severe emotional outbursts and breakdowns. Everything sent her into an uncontrollable emotional mess. Naturally, we figured it was P/P. We had her tested and found there was strep, but we decided to heal the C. diff first. Since starting her on homeopathic treatment, we have had fewer outbursts and she's had a lot more confidence. Her tic (uncontrollable throat clearing) is gone. Our next step is to address the strep once we know that the C. diff is gone.

Now that we've healed some of Nick's bigger symptoms, I feel like we're connecting with him in a way that we couldn't before. I see more and more of my husband and me in him. He has my smart mouth and interest in technology, and my husband's love of biographies and Legos.

My biggest advice to other parents is to listen to your intuition and keep digging and researching. If I had heeded all the advice we had gotten early on, our kids wouldn't be on the road to healing right now. Also, make sure to find a practitioner knowledgeable in P/P and connect with other parents. Truly, only other parents and professionals who are familiar with P/P can understand the stress, anxiety and fear that go along with having a child with these diseases.

Thanks to a Friend

MOM, MARYLAND

From the time he was born, Ben had a happy-go-lucky temperament. He was laid-back and loved being with people. He laughed a lot and adored his two older brothers, who would read to him and play with him. School was a source of ease. Ben read at an early age and wrote creative stories that were pages long, filled with vocabulary that was beyond his age level. Advanced math came easy, too.

When Ben was in 3rd grade, we started hearing from his teacher that he wasn't paying attention in class, had some hyperactivity and was sometimes irritable. We weren't overly concerned. The issues—like interrupting the teacher or not wanting to participate in groups—were fairly minor and could be explained away by the fact that he was simply an ever-changing growing boy.

When 4th grade came along, there was an increase in schoolwork refusal. Entire worksheets were left blank. Ben, once a confident reader, refused to read aloud. He seemed to be in a brain fog, unable to express himself well. He was shutting down, and anger started creeping in. He would hit things; one time he flipped over a desk at school. We started him on ADHD medication and play therapy. While we saw some small improvements, the play therapist was not really able to connect with Ben.

By 5th grade, Ben's work refusal increased. His handwriting became sloppy and his math skills declined. He was getting bloody noses daily. He looked unhappy and irritable all the time. His desire to read went away completely, and he lost organizational skills.

My husband and I were exhausted trying to figure out how to help him. We could see this was more than ADHD. My two older sons have ADHD and anxiety, but the traditional forms of treatment worked well for them and they are now thriving young men. This was different. For my other boys, setting expectations worked. Having clear consequences worked. Positive reinforcement charts worked. Not for Ben. He didn't understand consequences because most of the time he didn't know why he was doing what he was doing. Consequences after meltdowns were pointless; he couldn't even remember what had happened.

He was losing friends, too, and he knew it. He was no longer invited to friends' houses or parties. He became a loner. We added psychiatric prescriptions to the mix with minimal improvement. At times the medication seemed to make things worse. With the medication came hallucinations and increased irritability. I felt hopeless, angry and scared of the future for myself, our family and my marriage.

Everything came crashing down in the 6th grade. I was

getting calls at least twice a week that I needed to pick up Ben from school. He would throw things. The work refusal was at its peak. He was diagnosed with dysgraphia. Math skills declined further. He talked about hating certain people. He was anxious and paranoid, sure that people were out to get him. Finally, in February of that year, the school called the police and wanted to take him to the ER for a mental health evaluation. As a registered nurse I knew how the ER might handle his situation. I pulled Ben out of school, to the staff's relief. We got medical authorization to do at-home learning for the rest of the year.

Around this time my husband and I went to counseling to learn how to be better parents for a child with mental illness. However, the skills we learned were useless. Then, a friend of mine, whose child had P/P, suggested I have Ben evaluated. I started researching. We found a functional medicine doctor who treats P/P and she helped us uncover Ben's underlying issues, including Lyme disease, mold and mycoplasma. She also officially diagnosed Ben with P/P. We started treatment with antibiotics and supplements to address the Lyme disease and saw some gains. Soon after, we decided to wean Ben off the psychiatric medications and noticed a lift in his mood and a decrease in his anxiety.

When Ben entered the 7th grade I decided to homeschool him myself. I felt he didn't have the support he needed at school. The pandemic had hit, and the school was not returning to in-person learning anyway. Homeschooling any child is challenging, but with a P/P child it's even more so. Thankfully, Ben was able to learn at his own pace. He was doing better, but still not great. I knew he needed something else, but didn't know what. Even with my traditional nursing background, I've always believed in alternative medicine. We came across homeopathy and decided to give it a go.

Within months of starting homeopathy, Ben returned to his 7th-grade classroom. He has friends and is enjoying the things he used to do. He's aware of his illness and recognizes how he has improved. Most of his ADHD symptoms are gone. He is getting straight A's and is confident and social. He can make his own lunch. He plays with his dogs. He is enjoying reading again. His math skills are back. We still see some occasional irritability, but he has not had a true terrible flare in months. Is P/P gone? Probably not. But he is thriving. And we have hope for his future.

P/P can and will suck the life out of you. The isolation of being a P/P parent is cold and lonely. Medical professionals look at you like you're crazy and many refuse to look outside the box. There are so many components: for the child, for the siblings and for the parents. The layers go deep. The strain that P/P can put on a marriage is real. I'm blessed to have an amazing husband and we went and are going through this together. Siblings suffer. They don't understand and are resentful because time is taken away from them to handle the ever-changing issues. The P/P child's behavior is annoying, frustrating and confusing for everybody in the family.

What have I learned? Without you, the parent, your child will not heal. You have to think outside the check-marked boxes, trust your gut, and lean on your spouse, if you have one, for support. When your child is in a flare, remember why it's happening. Don't assume the behavior is intentional. Seek therapy for yourself. I started Eye Movement Desensitization and Reprocessing (EMDR) therapy, and it has been my saving grace. I'm able to handle situations better, am less stressed and am finding hope for the future. I do believe my son can sense my feelings, fear and happiness. Once I was able to have less fear, things got better.

The trauma is real. Don't overlook what you need. Ground yourself to provide a stable foundation for yourself and family. Become your own rock first, and the rest will follow.

Pickles, Pepsi and Persistence

Mom, Delaware

Our son, Jonathan, was born with his dad's easygoing temperament. By age 2 he knew how to use a computer, was potty-trained and was articulate beyond his years—so much so that he started preschool that year.

Then, in 2003, at age 5, Jonathan complained of a sore throat. Within a day or two we took him to see his pediatrician. The staff performed the usual rapid strep test, gave us a prescription for an antibiotic, and instructed us to start him on it. They said they'd call us with the results of the overnight culture. When they called, they told us he didn't in fact have strep and that we could discontinue the antibiotic. That was the worst thing we ever did. Soon after, we put Jonathan to bed one night, just as we had every other night of his life, and the next day he awoke a different child. That's when our story, or should I say nightmare, began.

Jonathan started exhibiting signs of anxiety, OCD and a tic. He constantly had to be by my side, suffering from intense separation anxiety. His OCD presented itself as

157

repeating. He asked us to repeat anything and everything we said. Can you imagine what it was like to remember what you said five minutes ago while having an everyday conversation with him or another family member? We would make things up (because we couldn't remember) but he knew that was not what we had said. He couldn't move on until he was satisfied with our answers. He also constantly cleared this throat. Whether he was eating, drinking or doing neither, he cleared his throat. Between these three symptoms, we felt like we were going crazy (or he was). Worse, we knew our little boy wasn't himself and we didn't know why.

His pediatrician was stumped. My husband searched the Internet frantically day and night to determine what he had. Was it Tourette's syndrome or did Jonathan now suffer from OCD? We had no clue what had transformed him overnight. Meanwhile, I tried locating a pediatric psychiatrist who could see him immediately. I found one, but he couldn't see us for weeks. That just wasn't acceptable. I explained our situation to the scheduler, and along with some desperate begging and pleading, she squeezed us in.

I can't recall how many times we saw this psychiatrist, but during one of the visits, he recommended we try a psychiatric medication, an antidepressant, for treating the OCD. We did that, and our world turned even more upside-down. After only one dose, Jonathan talked about killing himself. Remember—Jonathan was only 5 years old—and he told us how he was going to do it (with the kitchen knives). You can imagine how distraught we were and concerned for his safety. We did not give him any additional doses and stopped seeing the psychiatrist.

At the recommendation of a friend, we took Jonathan to a hospital that was known for transferring patients to a local psychiatric hospital. We thought we might be able to find some answers there. We were willing to try almost anything. We went to the hospital, but because our son wasn't suffering from a life-threatening injury or illness, we spent most of the day waiting to be seen. We made it as far as a gurney in the hallway. A young nurse met with us and we explained our son's situation to her. We told her why we picked this particular hospital. After listening, she strongly recommended against asking a doctor to send him to the psychiatric hospital for evaluation. She said that we, his parents, would not be allowed in, only Jonathan. Upon her advice, we did not pursue the referral. We left, once again not knowing where to turn.

At this time, our son attended daycare in the morning and kindergarten in the afternoon. When I'd drop him off at daycare, he would suffer from terrible anxiety. He insisted I carry a notebook and pen with me and write down everything he said, like the exact time I would be picking him up. On the days I'd take him to kindergarten, he'd leave the classroom and try to run after me. Once, he chased my van. Luckily, I just happened to be looking in my rearview mirror and saw him. These situations were now becoming a regular part of our daily life. It was impossible to try to explain to Jonathan's daycare and kindergarten teachers what was going on, when we ourselves didn't know. They looked at us like we had three heads. Thankfully, the school principal was understanding and did all he could to help us get Jonathan through each day.

Social events were now an issue, too. Going to a friend's birthday party caused anxiety for him and stress for us. He just couldn't interact with other children like he used to. We started avoiding all social events except those with family.

Then, one day, we turned a corner. The pediatrician called and suggested we see a neurologist. The neurologist started out by examining Jonathan while my husband filled her in on what diagnoses he suspected through his Internet searches—one of which was PANDAS.

She said that she, too, believed he was suffering from PANDAS. She said PANDAS wasn't very well accepted in the medical community at the time. She recommended a strong dose of a particular antibiotic for a two-week period. Because the antibiotic's taste was so strong, Jonathan couldn't stand it. He had recently started eating pickles and we had just discovered a new brand of spicy pickles that made him want to drink something after. We would give him the spicy pickle and then he'd drink the antibiotic mixed with Pepsi.

After the two-week course of antibiotics, Jonathan returned to us. The anxiety, OCD and tic all stopped. Just as it came, it went. We then had his tonsils removed, and he never got strep infections after that. Today our son is 22. Even now when he gets a sore throat, we panic. Will it return? No one knows.

Since his recovery, Jonathan has been an exemplary student. He recently graduated from college summa cum laude. While in college he became a published scientific author and was nominated as his class valedictorian. He is now attending medical school.

If your child complains of a sore throat, get them to their pediatrician and have a strep test done immediately. Don't ignore that your child "just" has strep. Strep is a serious infection and shouldn't be taken lightly. If your child wakes up one morning a different child than they have always been, take them to their pediatrician and mention P/P. If your pediatrician dismisses you, find a doctor who will listen. Time is of the essence, and if you are able to get a diagnosis and begin a treatment plan as soon as possible, the effects could possibly be reversed, like in the case of Jonathan.

We know that having a child with P/P takes a toll on everyone in the family. As tough as times may get, remember, tomorrow is another day—a day filled with possibility and hopefully, a day when your former child returns. There isn't a day that goes by that we are not thankful to God, the doctors, nurses, teachers, principal and everyone else who helped us along the way, and of course, those spicy pickles!

Closing Thoughts, Parent to Parent

If our children's healing were the direct result of doctor's appointments, school meetings, therapy sessions, late-night research, lab draws, superhuman patience, advocacy, medications, supplements, calming techniques, money, tears and/or sheer exhaustion, our children would already be completely healed. But, as one of the moms said so eloquently in her story, healing is a sacred and complex process that takes time. One of the biggest emotional burdens of loving and caring for a child with P/P is not knowing when things will get better. And harder yet, not being able to tell your suffering child when things will get better. If these disorders came with an expiration date, or even a things'll-get-slightly-more-tolerable date, oh how much easier it would be to endure them.

A study conducted at Stanford University's PANS clinic measured the caregiver burden for about 100 parents of children with PANS (Farmer, et al., 2018). Most of the study's participants had a fairly high socioeconomic status. The study examined five categories of caregiver burden:

time dependency, emotional health, physical health, development and social relationships. A common benchmark for defining caregiver burden for an adult taking care of another adult is a score of 36, with scores above 36 indicating a high risk of burnout. The median score of the P/P parents in the study was 37, slightly higher than caring for an Alzheimer's patient. Alzheimer's! And these are parents whose children are being treated at a PANS clinic. How much higher would the scores be for families who have yet to find a practitioner. Or whose children continue to get misdiagnosed.

Yet only two families in the study reported hiring formal respite care. The study's authors wrote, "Some insurance policies, including Medicare, pay for limited respite care for caregivers of patients who qualify for hospice. Caregivers of patients with Alzheimer's Disease would qualify. To our knowledge, no PANS families qualify for respite care covered by insurance."

With such a high caregiver burden, taking care of ourselves, in whatever ways are remotely feasible, becomes a necessity, not a luxury. I remember seeing a therapist a few months after the onset of our son's symptoms. Thankfully, she was very familiar with P/P. I sunk down into the chair, feeling physically and mentally weighed down from the realities of our new life. As we began to talk, she gently asked me, "What kind of self-care are you doing?" I stared at her blankly. This was no time for a bubble bath. Our son was a stranger to us, and our life was crumbling. I could barely leave his side; the thought of "me time" seemed truly impossible.

She stared at me earnestly. "Whatever coping mechanisms and self-care you've used to get you to this point in your life won't be enough anymore. You have a child with special needs now." She talked to me about making a plan to do something for myself. I tried to focus, but all I cared about was figuring out how to help my child; I'd have time to rest later. And yet she was so adamant that I listened. I went home and actually did start a bath, thinking there was no way I wouldn't get interrupted by a rage or other crisis. Thankfully, my husband was able to keep our son from coming into the bathroom. I sat down in the tub and just cried.

Now, a couple years later, I understand why of all topics, that is the one she emphasized so much. As much as we want this healing process to be an all-out sprint to the end, it is a marathon, and one we need to pace ourselves for. You know yourself: what brings you joy and what steals it. You might need to exercise more than you ever have; you might need to exercise less than you ever have. You might need to lean heavily on your friends or put some friendships on the back burner for a bit. You might need to savor moments of quiet by getting up earlier or staying up later than the rest of your household. Let go of as much guilt as possible. Talk to other families a little farther ahead on the journey. Ask for help from family and friends; most want tangible ways to be there for you. Say no to as many unnecessary things vying for your time and energy as you possibly can; there's a time and a place to volunteer for a PTA position—now is *not* the time. Don't underestimate the power of having a good hiding place for your chocolate. Squeeze the joy out of absolutely anything and everything you can. (All of this and double for single parents!)

I asked the families in this book what mantras or thoughts helped them stay positive during the most difficult times, and these are some they shared:

◊　I will not give up until my child is free of this illness.

◊　Our love will not falter.

◊　I am stronger than I know.

◊　It's not [child's name]. It's PANS/PANDAS.

◊　I woke up today. I'm doing it. This is not my forever.

◊　We CAN and WILL get through this.

◊　Tomorrow is a new day.

◊　True healing takes time.

◊　There is grace for all of us.

◊　I have been assigned this mountain to show others it can be moved.

As you go forward, know that the P/P journey can feel like one gigantic puzzle. You open the box to solve it and— *What.* Where the $#&% are the pieces?! Unfortunately, this puzzle requires you to go out and find each piece, here, there and everywhere. And every so often a whole section you've been working on snaps into place, and you can almost see how beautiful the picture's going to look at the end. Other times you've been working on the puzzle for months and suddenly it feels like someone just threw all the edge pieces in the trash. But the truth is, you are always moving forward. Every discovery, every observation, every epiphany, every treatment that does or doesn't work leads to the next piece. When something doesn't work, that's not a failure of time and resources; it's a clue to finding the next piece that will help. And we can all find strength and encouragement knowing that countless P/P families and practitioners have worked tirelessly to make sure those pieces are easier to find than when they first went looking for them.

Don't forget to take deep breaths and celebrate every small and big victory. Every small victory IS a big victory. Our children are incredible examples of bravery, resilience, determination and inner strength. Their struggles are not in vain. What they will work through and overcome as kids and teenagers will make them even more empathetic, determined and caring adults.

And one day, it will hit you. Your family is having more good days than bad. You know what stuff helps. You know what doesn't. Your child is laughing again. Doing the things they used to love. Trying things you never thought they'd try. Overcoming what used to be insurmountable. Are there still hard moments, hard days, hard nights? Yes. But you've gotten through harder ones. And the hard times seem to pass more quickly, and the joyful times last longer. And then you'll find yourself remembering where you were, holding out your hand to another family still in the deep, and reminding them that their child is in there, too, somewhere.

Hugs,

Melissa

Acknowledgements

Thank you, from the bottom of my heart, to all the families who so willingly and generously shared your experiences for this book. From the beginning, this book felt like a quilt, with each of your stories making up the squares. Without one, there would have been an unmistakable hole. Thank you for your patience and allowing me to ask you so many questions. I know it was hard to relive those memories, and yet each of you did it with honesty and vulnerability, for the sole purpose of helping others. I know that families reading your stories will be able to relate to some part of your journey and will see their family in yours. I hope that sharing your story in this way helped your healing, too.

Thank you to the children who shared their art and stories, especially Delaney Atkinson, who created the gorgeous artwork for the front cover. You are all PANS and PANDAS warriors. Your creativity, whether through words or art, helped paint a more complete picture of what it's like to live with these disorders. There is no doubt in my mind, that, just as the quote at the start of the book says, you will each become a sun on the next traveler's horizon.

Thank you to our families—the grandparents, aunts and

uncles of our children who have supported us and encouraged us every step of the way. Your unconditional love has meant everything. We are so, so lucky.

To my husband, Joe: Well before we had a name for what was happening to our child, we were faced with the hardest chapter of our lives. When I think of how we got through it, I know exactly how: We never blamed each other. It was always us against whatever this was. When one of us was at a low, all it took was a look, and the other would step in. Every single trauma and triumph we experienced together. So many tears and so many hugs. It got to the point where we could exchange paragraphs of thoughts and emotion with a single look. You really are the heart of our family. I love how you always bring us together as one family team. You have an amazing way of speaking to our children, of encouraging them, giving them confidence, and applauding their uniqueness. I am so thankful they get to grow up in a household where their dad honors, respects and loves their mom so well. I love you.

Candice, thank you for being the first one to always remind me how amazing your nephew is. You remind me what is important, and what isn't. What to spend energy on and what not to. You are an amazing listener. You remind me that every person has a different path, and that his path will be incredible because of who he is. Your perspective and insights always come from a place of love and care for all of us. I'm also so grateful for your help in editing this book. Your suggestions and feedback were invaluable, and your enthusiasm for the book truly helped me get to the finish line.

Leslie, aside from those living in our house, there's not a person who has experienced more of our P/P journey than you. Your family has been a constant source of support. From Day 1, you never judged. Never questioned. Always listened. Always cried with me. Wherever I was: On my doorstep. In my car. On my couch. You always lifted me up. Brought me something yummy to eat. Made me laugh when I thought I couldn't. And now you celebrate each of his victories as if he were your own child. Thank you will never be enough.

Jamie, after 33 years of friendship, there are no filters. When one of us is hurting, the other feels it. When one of us celebrates an achievement, the other is cheering the loudest. When something, anything, happens, I have to tell you. Thank you for feeling all the ups and downs with me. For reminding me just how far he has come. For reminding me how far he will go. For making me laugh like no one else can. There's a reason my kids call you Aunt Jamie. They love you like I love you.

Amanda, I've never met someone who truly never judges anyone else. You always remind me of the good and the positive. I treasure your gentle wisdom. No matter what you have going on, you always have time to listen, to help me process and to orientate my heart. From the beginning you encouraged me to trust my gut and make choices that felt right to us, even if they weren't the traditional paths. For that and for so many other reasons, I'm so thankful for our friendship.

Jan, Christina and Jen: I'll forever remember falling asleep mid-morning after a particularly hard night. I woke up to muffled sounds of talking outside and opened the blinds. There sat the three of you, and Les, on our curb, praying for our family. Thank you each for reminding me of the importance of prayer and pointing me toward God always. Your friendship has meant the world.

Deb, I will never forget when we were connected. I could barely leave the house and I arrived late at the restaurant to meet you. "I knew it would be hard for you to get out of the house," you told me. "I would have waited here all night." During that first conversation, you said, "We're going to get your child back." You were the first person to give me hope. I clung to the confidence of your words. I'm so thankful that we got to help each other with our books and that we get to cheer on each other's children. The P/P world is lucky to have you.

To those educators who went above and beyond when school anxiety was so high: Joe and I will always be grateful for your empathy, understanding and flexibility. Ms. Doffing and Ms. Horner, two of the best teachers we've ever known: From visiting him on our front lawn, coming out to our car in the mornings, offering to rollerblade with him to school (!), allowing me to talk to the class about P/P, and cheering on his every success, you did everything you could (and more) to provide a safe, loving environment. Ms. Ramrez, thank you for your guidance, ideas, kindness, empathetic ear and all those Minecraft chats! Ms. Cartlidge, you are everything a principal should strive to be. Your positivity and the way you prioritize and support students, teachers and parents is just amazing.

Dr. Griesemer, thank you for writing the beautiful introduction to this book, and being that caring therapist who encouraged me to prioritize self-care. I carry your words with me, and I'm honored to have you be part of this book.

Thank you to all the fellow P/P moms I have become close with (some of whom I've never met in person). I admire each of you and I'm so thankful for our friendship: Claudia, Monica, Shari, Laura M., Tarita, Laura N., Emily, Tandra, Tiffany and so many more.

Lastly, to our children: Your dad and I can't promise that we will be perfect parents; you already know that we are not. All we can promise is that you will always, always, be deeply loved and cherished. We hope that the past four years especially have shown you that we will always get through everything together, as a team. You may not always feel like things are fair—that your sibling gets more than you do. You will each need different things throughout your childhood, and we promise we will always give each of you what you, in particular, need to thrive, when you need it. We will always listen to you; you both have so much wisdom to share. Thank you for raising us to be better parents.

For More Information

VISIT

PANDAS Network (www.pandasnetwork.org)

The Foundation for Children with Neuroimmune Disorders (www.neuroimmune.org)

Aspire Care (www.aspire.com)

PANDAS Physicians Network (www.pandasppn.org)

WATCH

My Kid Is Not Crazy (via Amazon Prime Video)

Stolen Childhood (via YouTube or Amazon Prime Video)

READ

The Parent's Survival Guide to PANDAS/PANS. Marcus, Deborah. Seedfire Publishing, 2021.

Saving Sammy: A Mother's Fight to Cure Her Son's OCD. Maloney, Beth Alison. Broadway Books, 2010.

Brain Under Attack: A Resource for Parents and Caregivers of Children with PANS, PANDAS, and Autoimmune Encephalitis. Lambert, Beth et al., Answers Publications, 2018.

About the Author

Melissa Nolan lives in Austin, TX, with her husband, two children and beagle/cocker spaniel mix Queso, who, despite lacking official therapy dog certification, has brought immeasurable healing to her whole family.

She earned her journalism degree from Cal Poly, San Luis Obispo, and now works in accounting (go figure).